AF651468

ENCYCLOPAEDIA OF EMINENT THINKERS

VOLUME-X: **M.N. ROY**

Encyclopaedia of Eminent Thinkers Series

Vol. I. The Political Thought of **Mahatma Gandhi**
Vol. II. The Political Thought of **Nehru**
Vol. III. The Political Thought of **Rabindra Nath Tagore**
Vol. IV. The Political Thought of **Radhakrishnan**
Vol. V. The Political Thought of **Vinoba**
Vol. VI. The Political Thought of **Aurobindo**
Vol. VII. The Political Thought of **Jayaprakash Narayan**
Vol. VIII. The Political Thought of **Vivekananda**
Vol. IX. The Political Thought of **Ambedkar**
Vol. X. The Political Thought of **M.N. Roy**

About the Author

K.S. Bharathi did his Master's Degree in Gandhian Thought, Peace-Science, Economics, and Political Science. He also did Postgraduate Diplomas in Politics, Public Administration, Population Dynamics, Gandhian Thought, Tourism, and Telgu. He has contributed some articles in learned journals. He is the author of : *Foundation of Gandhian Thought, Gandhi and Humanity, Socio-Religious Thoughts of Mahatma Gandhi, The Philosophy of Sarvodya, The Satyagraha of Mahatma Gandhi, Gandhi and Nehru, Foundations of Ambedkar Thought, The Social Philosophy of Mahatma Gandhi, Gandhian Approach to Rural Development, The Relevance of Gandhi, Gandhi and Vinoba, The Philosophical Foundations of Gandhian Thought, The Political Thought of Gandhi, The Economic Thought of Gandhi, The Social Thought of Gandhi,* and *The Quintessence and Chronology of Gandhi*. At present, he is the Head of the Postgraduate Department of Gandhian Thought of Nagpur University. He is the Chairman of the Board of Studies of Gandhian Thought, member of the Academic Council, member of the Faculty of Social Sciences, member of the Board of Examination, and member of the Doctoral Research Committee of Nagpur University.

ENCYCLOPAEDIA OF EMINENT THINKERS SERIES-10

VOLUME-TEN

THE POLITICAL THOUGHT OF M.N. ROY

K.S. BHARATHI
Head, P.G. Dept. of Gandhian Thought,
Nagpur University, Nagpur

CONCEPT PUBLISHING COMPANY, NEW DELHI - 110059

All rights reserved. No part of this work may be reproduced, stored in a retrieval system, or transmitted in any form or by any means, electronic, mechanical, photocopying, microfilming, recording or otherwise, without the prior written permission of the copyright owner and the Publisher.

ISBN 81-7022-711-9 (Vol. 10)
ISBN 81-7022-684-8 (Series)

First Published 1998

© K.S. **Bharathi** (*b.* 1956)

Published and Printed by

Ashok Kumar Mittal
Concept Publishing Company
A/15-16, Commercial Block, Mohan Garden,
NEW DELHI - 110059 (India)

Phones: 5649024, 5648039

Fax 091-011-5648053

TO

MY DAUGHTER

K.B. PREETI

PREFACE

There are many valuable books on M N. Roy. There is hardly any book attempting a comprehensive exposition and evaluation of the political thought of M.N. Roy. This work seeks to provide a comprehensive exposition of the Political Thought of M.N. Roy in a lucid manner.

Roy was more a philosopher than a mass leader. He was essentially one of the greatest thinkers of the twentieth century and truly a citizen of the world. He was least concerned about himself and most of his life suffered due to a honest and straight forward approach to different national and international problems. His chief concern was to realise freedom for himself and for others.

Roy rejected both dictatorship of the proletariat and parliamentary democracy as the solution of the present problems. He was a passionate humanist. He was impressed by the philosophy of Karl Marx in the beginning of his political career. His socialism was founded on 'Kingdom of freedom'. He had faith in the creativity of man. He stressed the values of humanism as the basis of struggle for a higher form of society. He advocated scientific thinking and scientific politics free from any presupposition and dogma. He began his career as a politician but ended as a political teacher and philosopher. He was quite a complex character.

I would like to place on record my indebtedness to scholars and thinkers whose ideas enabled me to bring out this book. I gratefully acknowledge the scholars from whose works I have drawn citations viz. Dr. D.R. Bali, Dr. R.C. Gupta, Dr. V. Singh, Dr. V.D. Mahajan and Dr. Bhola Singh.

So far as the writing of this book is concerned, whatever success I have achieved is due to the relentless efforts and encouragement of my friend, philosopher and guide, Dr. P.S.G. Kumar, Head, Department of Library and Information Science, Nagpur University. I sincerely express my gratitude to him.

I am indebted to Mr. Ashok Kumar Mittal, Concept Publishing Company, for publishing this book in such a short span of time. Finally I hold myself to blame for the errors and shortcomings if any. This work would have not been completed without the grace of Lord Venkateswara of Tirumala and Alamelu Thayar of Tiruchanur.

K.S. BHARATHI

CONTENTS

1

LIFE AND WORK OF ROY

Narendra Nath Bhattacharya, later known by the assumed name of Manabendra Nath Roy, was born in a village, namely Arbalia in West Bengal on 21 March, 1887 in a priestly family. The priesthood in the family went by heredity. His grandfather, Bhairavananda Bhattacharya was the head-priest of the temple of Goddess Ksheputeshwari in the village Ksheput in the Midnapur district of West Bengal. His father, Pandit Dinabandhu Bhattacharya, was a school teacher and inherited the priest position. He received his early education in the village school. He studied up to class VI in Arbelia village school. He hardly had any formal education beyond the elementary schooling. In 1898, the family moved on to the Kodalia village. Here he studied at the Harinabhi Anglo-Sanskrit School. In his school days, he participated in various political activities of the national movement and later he became an active member of the revolutionary movement in Bengal. He joined the National College in Calcutta founded by Aurobindo Ghosh. Later he joined the Bengal Technical Institute in Calcutta and left it for ever. Yet he was essentially a self-educated man. Hary Kumar Chakravarthy said, "From boyhood Roy had a thirst for knowledge. He used to say, as a youngman, that knowledge is freedom and the urge for freedom is inherent in every man".[1]

To quote Professor Sibnarayan Ray, "As I think M.N. Roy, I believe, has his peers, if not in the East, certainly in the

West. But in the wealth of experience, which went into the shaping of his thoughts, he was altogether unique and had none to compare either in the past or in the present. From Socrates to Santayana, from Kung Fu-Tze to Croce, I know of no philosopher, who possessed his sweep of experience".[2] Professor G.D. Parikh said, "Manabendra Nath Roy was without a peer; there is, perhaps, no comparable figure in the East. He was unique in the universality of his experience. A dozen different countries spread over three major continents provide the background of his chequered career. He occupied leading positions in the great movements of *Nationalism, Communalism* and *Humanism*".[3]

Broadly speaking, Roy's biography can be divided in three stages. They are national Anarchism, Marxism and New Humanism. These stages, though different from each other, figure along a continuum of a thought process of organic growth and development. To Roy, Marxism only appealed as a mere convincing explanation for his innate human inquisitiveness. The driving force of his Marxism was his *Humanism*. Truth and *freedom* were not mere ideas to be professed but they were the ultimate realities of human life. He always corrected himself on the basis of his new experiences. He always fought for right cause, which he considered to be just. He said, "Lie-hunting is my profession. This is a thankless job. But someone must tell the truth, if it is not to remain an empty concept. I have been lie-hunting ever since I learnt to think for myself to distinguish facts from fictions. It has not won me popularity".[4]

To quote M.N. Roy's wife, Ellen Roy, "It should, however, not be thought that the phases mentioned above were sharply separated from one another or that there were any violent mutation in his life. Rather they led logically and naturally one to the other and were but stages in a process of organic growth and development. Roy never disavowed his past; to the end he acknowledged Jatin Mukherjee and Karl Marx to be his principal mentors—next in importance only to that greatest mentor of all, like itself ".[5] Throughout his life, he had pursued the quest for human freedom. He said, "When as a school boy of fourteen I began my political life, which may end in nothing. I wanted to be free... In those days we had not read Marx. We did not know about the existence of the *Proletariat*. Still, many spent their lives in jail and went to the gallows. There was no proletariat to propel them. They were not conscious of the class struggle. They did not have the dream of *Communism*. But they had the human urge to revolt against the intolerable conditions of life. They did not know exactly how these conditions could be changed. But they tried to change them, any how. I began my political life with that spirit, and I still draw my inspiration rather from that spirit than from the three volumes of Capital or three hundred volumes by the Marxists".[6]

According to one of Roy's coworkers, "Narendra almost a boy, hardly fourteen, and yet virile and energetic, full of *revolutionary* enthusiasm, rushed into a little room, in which we were holding an informal talk on the problems then facing us in Bengal and elsewhere. He had a talk with us. After this, he offered himself as a whole-timer for the cause of liberty of India from the foreign yoke. He declared on oath that he would be prepared to do the impossible; for, there was nothing impossible for revolutionary. Soon after, he joined us; he proved to be of very great value to our movement and possessed rare qualities found only in a great leader of men".[7]

Roy involved himself in *revolutionary* activity at an early age. In 1905, his life started taking a new and crucial turn. It was, among other eventful developments, the year of Bengal partition. He organised protests and demonstrations against partition in defiance of the order of the school's headmaster. He was rusticated from the school. He also joined a revolutionary organisation called Anushilan Samiti. He took particular interest in chemistry which was to be of great use shortly. He was one of the most trusted lieutenants of J.N. Banerjee. He was influenced by Bankim's *Anand Math* novel.

He said, "Bankim Chaterji's *Anand Math* was our common source of inspiration. Therein we found our revolutionary ideal. As a matter of fact, we had distributed amongst ourselves the roles of the prominent figures of that drama. They were *sanyasins*. We had taken the vow to follow in their foot-steps".[8]

Roy's activities went on expanding and acquiring clearer definition in revolutionary terms though, he engaged in extensive social and relief work. He chose his village itself for the promotion of revolutionary activities. He got together a small but close-knit underground revolutionary group and arranged for training in the needed skills such as practice in shooting and marksmanship. He now used his knowledge of chemistry to experiment with bomb-making and explosives. There was also to be faced the problem of maintaining the group of whole-time revolutionaries and of acquiring arms and *ammunition*. All this required a goodly sum of money not easy to get together. Political dacoity suggested itself as the most effective means of meeting this need.

For the first time, Roy was arrested in 1907 in connection with Chingripota political dacoity case. Once again he was arrested in connection with Howrah Conspiracy case in 1910. He participated in a number of other political *dacoities* and conspiracies, and got arrested, but was each time either acquitted for want of sufficient evidence or jumped bail. The famous Garden Reach dacoity which took place in 1915 in broad daylight was the work of his group under his leadership.

Roy and Jatin had several meetings with the German Counsel General in Calcutta to explore the possibility of enlisting German help and support for implementing the plan of armed insurrection. Secrets agents were sent to Germany to import arms and money from Germany. He left for Batavia in April 1915 under the Pseudonym Charles A. Martin. It was arranged with German Counsel in Batavia that the German cargoship would deliver the arms. He returned to India to make arrangements for receiving and unloading the arms and for despatching them to different countries. He made all the necessary arrangements but the ship did not arrive. Once again he went to Batavia and made new plans for the delivery and receipt of German arms. He failed this time in his mission. He did not return to India but went to Japan and from there to China. He concluded an agreement with a Chinese leader for the sale of arms to be delivered on the Indian frontier in the tribal area of Assam. He then saw the German Ambassador in Peking. The German Ambassador advised Roy to go to Germany to secure the necessary funds from the German General Staff in Berlin. He said, "Having spent a year and a half wandering through Malaya, Indonesia, Indo-China, the Philippines, Japan, Korea and China, in summer 1916, I landed at San Francisco".[9]

Roy arrived in San Francisco on 14 June, 1916. The news of his arrival found its way into the newspapers and came under police notice. This made it difficult for him to go about freely in San Francisco. He went to Pao Alto, the seat of the University of Stanford. He met Dhangopal Mukherji. On his advice, he changed his name to M.N. Roy. He met Evelyn Trent, an attractive graduate student. She was of radical views. They were married in New York. In New York, Roy met Lala Lajpat Rai. They became close friends. Roy studied the Marxian literature in the New York Public Library. He said, "It was not long before I accepted socialism, except its materialist philosophy. That was my last ditch, which I defended still for quite a long time".[10] This transition was a big event in his political life.

In 1917, Roy went to Mexico in order to avoid legal proceedings in connection with the Hindu-German conspiracy case. The Russian Revolution took place while he was in Mexico. It influenced him very much. He said, "I was sucked up in that electrified atmosphere. . . . It was a mutation in my political evolution: a sudden jump from die-hard nationalism to Communalism".[11] He joined the Mexican Socialist group, became its propaganda secretary and worked hard for its growth and expansion and succeeded in greatly augmenting its membership. This resulted in the formation of Mexican Socialist Party in December 1918. He became the general secretary of the Party. Michael Borodin came to see Roy. The two soon became close friends. There were frequent discussions between Roy and Borodin in Mexico and Roy became a full-fledged communist. Regarding Borodin influence, Roy said, "He initiated me in the intricacies of Hegelian Dialectics as the key to Marxism. My lingering faith in the special genius of India faded as I learned from him the history of European Culture".[12]

Roy was invited to the Second Congress of the Communist International in Moscow. He also received an invitation from Lenin. He left for Moscow in November 1919. He made personal acquaintance with important communist leaders. He contacted the members of the Indian Revolutionary Committee in Berlin. He had prepared a manifesto to put before the Communist International. He said, "What I learned during my several month's stay in Germany about the conditions in Europe and their immediate perspective fostered in me the feeling that the proletariat in the metropolitan countries would not succeed in their heroic endeavour to capture power unless imperialism was weakened by the revolt of the colonial peoples".[13] He left Berlin for Moscow in April 1920. He met Miss Angelica Balabanova, the first General-Secretary of the Communist International. She gave him a copy of the thesis written by Lenin on the national and colonial questions for discussion at the Second Congress. She conveyed him to see Lenin after some time. He met Lenin on the same day.

Roy had some basic difference with Lenin on national and colonial questions thesis. He submitted the supplementary thesis at the instance of Lenin. Both the documents were presented before the Congress and the Congress adopted both with some amendments. It was accepted to support only revolutionary movements of liberation, rather than all bourgeois—democratic liberation movements, as stated in the original draft. It was an original contribution of Roy. This was a land-mark in the history of Indian Political thought. He believed that the leadership of the Indian nationalist movement should be in the hands of the Proletariat. He was elected to the Presidium of the Communist International. His career in the *Communist International* began almost with a bang. He was from then on engaged in extensive and varied revolutionary and progressive activities and rose high within a short time in the hierarchy of international communism. He was appointed a member of the Central Asiatic Bureau of the Communist International at Tashkent. He gave training to a group of Muslim Muhajirins at Tashkent. He tried to raise an army of liberation in Tashkent and established an Indian Military School. He was instrumental in establishing an emigre Communist Party of India in Tashkent in October 1920. He became Head of the Eastern Department of the Communist International and of Moscow Oriental University.

The aim of Indian Military School in Tashkent was to train an army for Indian liberation. Roy said, "My plan was to raise, equip and train such an army in Afghanistan. Using the frontier territories as the base of operation and with the mercenary support of the tribesmen, the liberation army would march into India and occupy some territory, where a civil government should be established as soon as possible".[14] He came back to Moscow and founded the Communist University for the Toilers of East in 1922. He himself was its Director. By 1926 he had reached an enviable position in the Communist International. His passage to eminence was not smooth. He had to move from country to country, shifting his headquarters from one to the other, getting expelled by the government of the country to which he went, even before he had time to settle down there. A.K. Hindi said, "He was expelled from one country after another. He could not find refuge either in Switzerland, Sweden, Norway, Holland, Germany, Belgium, France or any other country ruled and governed by the capitalist classes".[15]

In 1920, Roy wrote *What Do We Want, The Problems of India, India in Transition* books. In 1922, *One Year of Non-Co-operation, The Future of Indian Politics* and *Political Letters* were published. He critically analysed the Indian society and the perspective of the development of the Indian national movement, from Marxian point of view. He had established a wide network of revolutionary contacts in India to develop a communist movement in the country.

Roy was sent to China in 1927 as head of a delegation of the Communist International to advise the Communist Party of China. A new thesis was adopted regarding China and he was sent to organise action according to the new line. He said, "The meeting of the Executive Committee of the Communist International in November 1926 adopted a new thesis on the Chinese question, the central point of which was that the Chinese Revolution must from that time be developed as an agrarian revolution. The leadership of the Chinese Communist Party as well as the representatives of the Communist International in China were of a different view. They still maintained that the nationalist bourgeoisie should be helped to lead the revolution and class struggle should not be accentuated for the sake of national unity. I was alone to advocate the different point of view that the Chinese Revolution had reached a critical moment in which it must strike out a new course and a fetish should not be made of the alliance with the Kuo Min Tang. The Executive of the Communist International adopted my point of view, which was opposed in the beginning by Stalin himself. But Stalin was brought around to my view and the thesis adopted by the ECCI was drafted by me. Immediately afterwards, I left for China".[16] His China Mission failed and he returned to Moscow in September 1927.

According to Roy, *decolonisation* takes place when there arises crisis in the capitalism and imperialism. He remarked, "When imperialism forced by its inner contradiction, permits, even encourages partial industrialisation of colonial country the basis of antagonism between bourgeoisie and foreign imperialism narrows down.... the native bourgeoisie outgrows the previous state of absolute colonial oppression".[17] After the First World War, the British imperialism had changed its strategy of exploitation of India. It began to industrialise the colony and giving concessions to the Indian bourgeoisie. He said, "In the last analysis colonial possessions represent labour. If more labour could be employed in more fruitful processes of production, the colonial exploitation would be more profitable. Land as a means of production was exhausted. Therefore, the interest of imperialism in crisis, of capitalism in decay, necessitated the introduction of other means of production than land in the colonial countries. That process was 'Decolonisation".[18]

Roy was held responsible for the Communist failure in China. He was also criticised for advocating the theory of decolonisation. Officially, he was expelled from the *Communist International* in September 1929. He stayed one more year in Berlin and wrote his work, *Revolution and Counter-Revolution in China*. He left for India and reached Bombay in the middle of December, 1930. He met some trade union leaders. He met Jawaharlal Nehru and went to attend the Congress Session at Karachi in March 1931. In July 1931, he was arrested in connection with Kanpur Conspiracy case. He defended himself before the Magistrate. He maintained that the British rule in India was not a legally established rule and that, therefore, an attempt to overthrow it was not illegal. He remarked that the only law for the oppressed and exploited people of India was the law of revolt, the majestic law of revolutionary struggle for *freedom*. He was convicted and sentenced to twelve years transportation. The sentence was later reduced by the High Court to one of six years rigorous imprisonment.

During his jail period, Roy studied very deeply philosophy and science. Regularly he sent letters to Ellen

Gottschalk. In 1943, all those letters were published in book form entitled *Letters from Jail*. After serving his six years term in various jails, he was finally released on 20 November, 1936 from jail in Dehradun. He brought out with him nine closely hand-written volumes and most part of it was later published in the form of books as *Fascism: Its Philosophy, Professions and Practice, Historical Role of Islam, Materialism, Heresies of Twentieth Century, Ideal of Indian Womanhood,* and others. From jail, he also wrote several letters to the leaders of the Indian National Congress. He had kept close contact with Ellen Gottschalk through letters from jail during the years of his incarceration arrived in India to join him in the pursuit of the common cause. They were married on 10 March, 1937 in Bombay.

Roy joined the Indian National Congress in November 1936. In December 1936, he attended the Annual Session of the Indian National Congress at Faizpur. He became a member of the A.I.C.C. He launched a weekly journal, *Independent India* on 4 April, 1937 from Bombay and in 1949 it was changed to *Radical Humanist*. He wanted to transform the Congress into a mass political party. He was a staunch critic of Gandhian leadership. He was not satisfied with the Gandhian group and so he established the League of Radical Congressmen to carry forward the word of activising and democraticing the Congress in May 1939. The Second World War broke out in September 1939 and he characterised it as a war waged by the Fascists against freedom. He wrote extensively on the issue of war in *Independent India*.

To propagate his ideas and action programme with a view to educating people, Roy was continually writing books, editing journals founded by himself and contributing to others. He was also the founder-editor of the quarterly journal of ideas, the *Humanist Way*. He launched the Radical Democratic Party in December 1940. To quote Professor B.N. Das Gupta, "Roy's Radical Democratic Party was the only section of Indian people, which held fast the view that this war would not only restore and re-establish democracy, but also incidentally liberate progressive forces all over the world. Roy used to go further than this and held the view that if the allies won, Labour Party would come to power in Britain and in that case, India would get Independence".[19] Indian Federation of Labour was organised under his guidance in November 1940.

Roy found no-where democracy in actual practice. He began to realise the inadequacies of *Marxism* and *Communism*. He said, "Neither Capitalism nor Communism was the answer to the situation. Capitalism had already proved its bankruptcy. Communism had also falsified all hopes. On the other hand, Communism held out the threat of a civil war on the national as well as on the international plane. It was, therefore, to go beyond Communism and evolve an ideology, a political structure and social institutions, which would ensure freedom as well as equality, security as well as free scope for development".[20] He realised that party politics was not conducive for democracy. He said, "I feel very uncomfortable in politics. I feel like a fish out of water. But having been drawn into this whirlpool since my early youth, I have not been able to get out of it. Perhaps, the time is coming when I shall at last do so".[21] He dissolved his own Radical Democratic Party in December 1948.

Roy founded the Indian Renaissance Institute at Dehradun. He was until his death its Founder-Director. One of the main objectives of the Institute was to undertake a study of Indian Culture and to evaluate old values in the light of modern knowledge and experience. He visualised the Institute growing into a twentieth century Nalanda University. It has remained a dream.

Roy wrote many books and pamphlets such as *From Savagery to Civilisation, Nationalism an Antiquated Cult, National Government or People's Government, Alphabet of Fascist Economics, People's Plan, Poverty or Plenty?, Planning New India, Constitution of Free India: A Draft, Problem of Freedom, Jawaharlal Nehru, Russian Revolution,*

New Orientation, New Humanism, Science and Philosophy. He elaborated the philosophy of Radical Humanism in 1948.

Roy wanted to bring about a philosophical revolution in the country. He remarked, "A political revolution or a social revolution presuppose a philosophical revolution. That is to say, the mentality of the people must change, that spirit of confirmism must go which upholds an established order, the predisposition to obey authority, the desire to follow blindly as the way of least resistance and least effort".[22] He devoted to the writing of the philosophy of *Radical Humanism*. The most important work that he wrote was *Reason, Romanticism and Revolution* in two volumes. He described the importance of philosophy of *New Humanism* in this book. He said, "New Humanism lays emphasis on the basic fact of history that man is the maker of his world—man as a thinking being, and he can be so only as an individual. The brain is the instrument of thought, and it is individually owned. It cannot be possessed collectively. Revolutions are heralded by iconoclastic ideas conceived by gifted individuals. A brotherhood of men attracted by the adventure of ideas, keenly conscious of the urge for freedom, fired with the vision of a free society of free men, and motivated by the will to remake the world, so as to restore the individual in his position of primacy and dignity, will show the way out of the contemporary crisis of modern civilisation. . . . New Humanism advocate a social reconstruction of the world as a commonwealth and fraternity of freedom, by the cooperative endeavour of spiritually emancipated moral men. New Humanism is cosmopolitan. A cosmopolitan commonwealth of spiritually free men will not be limited by the boundaries of national States—Capitalist, Fascist, Socialist, Communist, or any other kind—which will gradually disappear under the impact of the twentieth century Renaissance of man".[23]

Roy passed away at his Dehradun residence on 25 January, 1954. Tarka Teerth Laxman Shastri called him as "the first philosopher of modern India". He said, "The story of his life reads like an Epic, the concluding chapter of which constitutes a philosophy of life, integrating the fundamentals of science and the moral experience of Man".[24] To quote Jayaprakash Narayan, "In the death of M.N. Roy, India has lost one of her great sons. No one in modern India had such a long revolutionary life so full of drama and adventure. In the International Communist movement, he had held the highest position in the oriental section, and was the closest Asian associate of the great Lenin. When that movement began to degenerate into imperialistic expansionism, Roy had the rare courage, at the risk of his brilliant career and even his life, to oppose it at the highest levels. On his return to India, he had to suffer a long imprisonment. In recent years, he had retired from active politics, but had been doing path-breaking thinking. Not only India, but world society, needed at this movement his intellectual leadership".[25] Justice V.M. Tarkunde acknowledged him as a 'Prophet of a New Order'.

Both as a general theorist of revolution and as the historian of Russian revolution, Roy holds an important place among scholars and thinkers alike. But he did not succeed in comprehending the Indian revolutionary sense of conflict and reconstruction in terms of the concepts drawn from European thought and history. Radical Humanism occupies an important place in the growing tradition of modern Indian thought. Ever testing his thought in the light of experience and chastening his experiencing in the crucible of reason, he moved from terrorism and virulent Hindu nationalism to Marxism and Communism, from Communism to Radical Humanism, from formal democracy to humanist democracy, from internationalism to cosmopolitanism, thereby blazing a trail for those to come.

Roy neither equated freedom with national independence nor with the ending exploitation. *Freedom* to him had a wider meaning. It was the progressive disappearance of all restrictions on the unfolding of the potentialities of the individuals, as human beings, and not as cogs in the wheels of a mechanised social organism. His love of truth protected him all his life from the line of partisanship and dogmatism, narrow-mindedness and conformism.

REFERENCES

1. Usha Singh, *Economic Thought of Indian Socialists*, Deep & Deep Publications, New Delhi, 1985, p. 31.
2. Sibnarayan Roy, *M.N. Roy: Philosopher-Revolutionary*, Renaissance Publishers, Calcutta, 1959, p. 28.
3. M.N. Roy's Memoirs, *Introduction by G.D. Parikh*, Allied Publishers Private Limited, Bombay, 1964, p. v.
4. Sibnarayan Ray, *M.N. Roy: Philosopher-Revolutionary*, *op. cit.*, p. 4.
5. *The Radical Humanist*, 25-1-1956, p. 27.
6. M.N. Roy, *New Orientation*, Renaissance Publishers, Calcutta, 1946, p. 183.
7. A.K. Hindi, *M.N. Roy: The Man Who Looked Ahead*, The Modern Publishing House, Ahmedabad, 1938, p. 8.
8. *M.N. Roy's Memoirs, op. cit.*, p. 98.
9. *Ibid.*, p. 22.
10. *Ibid.*, p. 29.
11. *Ibid.*, p. 59.
12. *Ibid.*, p. 195.
13. *Ibid.*, p. 306.
14. *Ibid.*, p. 420.
15. A.K. Hindi, *M.N. Roy: The Man Who Looked Ahead*, *op. cit.*, p. 67.
16. M.N. Roy, *Revolution and Counter-Revolution in China*, Renaissance Publishers, Calcutta, 1946, p. 538.
17. R.K. Awasthi, *Scientific Humanism: Socio-Political Ideas of M.N. Roy: A Critique*, College Book Depot, Jaipur, p. 11.
18. M.N. Roy, *Scientific Politics*, Renaissance Publishers, Calcutta, 1947, p. 104.
19. B.N. Das Gupta, *M.N. Roy: Quest for Freedom*, Firma K.L. Mukhopadhyaya, Calcutta, pp. 11-12.
20. *M.N. Roy's Memoirs, op. cit.*, p. 600.
21. M.N. Roy, *New Orientation*, *op. cit.*, p, 59.
22. *The Radical Humanist*, 5-5-1968, p. 197.
23. M.N. Roy, *Reason, Romanticism and Revolution*, Vol. II, Renaissance Publishers, Calcutta, 1955, p. 310.
24. Sibnarayan Ray, M.N. Roy: Philosopher-Revolutionary, *op. cit.*, p. 13.
25. J.P. Narayan Papers, Subject File No. 622, Teen Murti House, Nehru Memorial Museum and Library, New Delhi.

2

SOURCES OF INSPIRATION

M.N. Roy can rightly be regarded as one of the forerunners of Indian Socialist Thought. While he is better known as a political philosopher, yet the economic content of his socialist ideas is no less important when considered in the context of the contemporary Indian perspective. He did not stick to any particular philosophy or school of thought.

Roy's ideas on economic problems and their solution are the bye-products of the transformation of his personality from time to time caused by his experiences and his personal contacts. He said, "The strongest impression I am carrying here from Europe is that Europe can't for any length of time sustain the artificial life its people are living today, because that life is too materialistic. There must be a return to simplicity and proper proportions. The flesh has gained precedence over the spirit. The machine age is ruling western civilisation. Poor *production* and lack of the means of proper distribution may finally spell the doom of capitalist society. The only solution I see is a return to hand industry and the emancipation of the individual from factory slavery".[1]

Roy looked upon a 'Labour Intensive Economy' based on the dignity of labour as the only solution for the exploited humanity. Regarding the *influence* and experience of his tours from country to country, Mr. B.N. Das Gupta said, "All these travels from 1919 to 1928, he (Roy) became not only a hard-boiled practical man—a man of the world but he also came in contact with numerous revolutionaries—men and women, poets, philosophers, diplomats, scientists and from the ordinary labourers to the highest aristocrats, administrators and generals. There is hardly a man who has travelled more and that so fruitfully and has seen more with eyes open, brain fully developed, mind receptive without any bias. The highest tribute is due to such a man".[2]

Roy recalls in his memoirs about the experiences in Mexico on the impact of Russian *revolution*. He said, "The Bolsheviks had just captured power in Russia, and a faint echo of the revolution reached across the Atlantic. All left-wing socialists were in an exuberant mood, and lived in an atmosphere surcharged with great expectations. They were all would be communists. I was sucked up in that electrified atmosphere. In my case, it was not a few degrees rise of the revolutionary temperature. It was a mutation in my political evolution, a sudden jump from die-hard nationalism to communism. With the fanaticism of a new convert reformism was an anathema".[3]

Roy had less opportunity to come in contact with eminent personalities from different walks of life. These contacts had shaped his ideas on *Socialism* and *Humanism*. He had his reservations about the individual in the shaping of his own destiny in the new set-up. To quote Grover, "Though Roy follows the original Soviet Plan in its people's committees with their right of recall, yet he checks the tendency of tiers of indirectly elected Soviets to become petrified and remote from the electorate by minimising the number of tiers and combining them with direct election of the Governor-General, the provincial governors and provincial People's Councils. The lowest People's Councils are very close to the rank and file as they number one in fifty of the adult population, and are elected annually. They participate continually in working of the government, and have the right of initiative".[4]

Roy could not agree with a system that rests on slavery under a sort of dictatorship in the garb of democracy as was the situation in Russia under Stalin. He could not compromise with the new developments in the post-revolution era and marked his break-away from Marxism. Das Gupta remarked, "When Roy found that his new political faith which was to have brought about world transformation and world emancipation degenerated into an instrument of enslavement of man, he, in his fury, pulled down his Master. He would have done better to remember that Marxism is a socio-economic tool or economic based political instrument for liberation of man from exploitation and to that extent only, it is a philosophy of life. He should have remembered that Lenin, Stalin, and he himself, were strategists when they were tackling Russian or Chinese problems—Lenin being the master-strategist as shown by his theory in his books and also by his performance. If Stalin failed to make his country free from exploitation and fear and failed to bring freedom of man, his failure did not indicate failure of Marx—there is nothing inherent in Marxism which inevitably precipitates towards totalitarianism".[5]

Roy's stay in Germany, Russia, China and Mexico afforded him to participate in revolutionary activities. Das Gupta observed, "Roy started as an anarchist and had a large share of revolutionary activities in Mexico, Germany, Russia and China. It was he who saw (as nobody else had the opportunity, equipment, courage and capacity of associating with revolutionary developments), the heroes of revolution, of fascism, of Nazism. He saw Russia starting with communism under Marxist leadership and ultimately developing into a *totalitarian state*, Roy's inner being revolted at the disappearance of freedom of man and of democracy of the state. His past association with Russia began to be galling and he not only condemned dictatorship of Stalin and the rest but he also lost the mental force out of disgust, dispair and disappointment. He began to make strong comments on Marxism and its Master which at times were out of proportion".[6]

Roy has his own convictions and originality of thought, yet he always respected the points of view of others. Das Gupta said, "In the case of Roy, revolutionary restlessness was in his blood and bones and still *freedom* and *democracy* permeated in his life. He was extremely intelligent but gullible to a degree and an optimist beyond a point. Roy was thus quite a complex character. The two strains—freedom and democracy on one side and revolutionary order on the other—in the same revolutionist is rare and history furnishes one other such example in Roza Luxemberg, one of the founders of German Communism. Roza was restless, far more unique and far more complex. On the other hand, Roy was quiet, reflective and intellectually absorbed".[7] Roy did not believe only in theoretical philosophy of Marxism.

It was a unique characteristic of Roy's personality that he gave deep thought to the problems and ideas that struck his mind. His analytical approach, impassionate reasoning and deep understanding kept him so absorbed that very often he was quite indifferent to his own surroundings and environments. He had founded the Radical Democratic Party in India with the sole objective to establish democracy after getting independence and make it an instrument for removal of poverty, social injustice and inequality and finally the emancipation of man not only in India but all over the world.

Roy had deep faith in Indian Nationalism. He accepted the drawbacks of Indian way of life such as caste system, religious superstitions, place of women in Indian society and the like. He advocated a progressive approach to socio-economic reform based on the application of modern science and technology.

REFERENCES

1. M.N. Roy, *India's Message: Fragment of a Prisioner's Diary*, Vol. 2, Renaissance Publisher Ltd., 1950, p. 222.
2. B.N. Das Gupta, *Quest for Freedom*, Firma K.L. Mukhopadhay, Calcutta, p. 8.

3. M.N. Roy's, *Memoirs,* Allied Publishers, 1964, p. 59.
4. D.C. Grover, *M.N. Roy: A Study of Revolution and Reason in Indian Politics*, Minerva Associates, Calcutta, 1973, p. 42.
5. B.N. Das Gupta, *Quest for Freedom, op. cit.*, pp. 39-40.
6. *Ibid.*, p. 39.
7. *Ibid.*, p. 42.

3

ROY ON PHILOSOPHY

M.N. Roy's view is dominated by his admiration for science and the scientific attitude. He knows that theories and principles formulated by science are not final. He believes in the unity of the sciences and of scientific method. Regarding the relationship between science and philosophy he said, "Science is a higher thing than philosophy. But philosophy needs not to be degraded, if it is conceived as the sum total of scientific knowledge".[1] "*Materialism* is vindicated as the only philosophy possible, provided that philosophy is defined as logical coordination of all the branches of positive knowledge in a system of thought to explain the world rationally and to serve as a reliable guide of life"[2] said Roy.

Roy's faith in science made him to lay stress that the universe is law-governed. Under the influence of Hegel, he interprets this fact as meaning that the universe is rational. The faith that the *universe* is law-governed has a crucial role in his philosophy of man. He does not agree with the interpretation of modern science. To him, probability itself is an expression of *Determinism*. The universe remains a system governed by mathematical laws that may be formulated with a high measure of exactitude.

The aim of Roy's philosophy is to rescue rationalism and ethics from the devastating consequences of scepticism. This is to be achieved within the framework of scientific materialism. The *mind* becomes conscious of the *environment*, the radius of which gradually expands until the entire nature is embraced. Human mind is necessarily rational in essence. He said, "The *mystery* of man has been solved by modern biology. Man is the outcome of biological evolution. In order to find the sanction of morality in man himself, and avoid at the same time the morass of mysticism, the roots of what is called conscience or moral sense must be traced in mechanistic biological functions.... The descent of man, therefore, can be traced to the law-governed physical universe. Man's rationality and moral sense, which are casually connected, are the expression of cosmic harmony".[3]

Roy is absolutely indifferent to religion. He is not agreeable to accept the dualistic ontology either of Kant or Descartes. So, he is called upon to account for the incidence of *freedom* in his law-governed universe. Man is something more than a part of nature. Nature is law-governed, knows no hesitation or conflict in its functionary under diverse circumstances. It suffers from no scruples or qualms of science. Man needs education, not only in logic and the sciences, but also in the apprehension and understanding of values, as also in wisdom or wise living, which involves judicious adjustment and ordering of diverse interests and values. His *philosophy* offers no explanation of the need on the individual's part to cultivate or educate his reason in its diverse forms.

During his stay in Russia, Roy came in close contact with professed followers of Marx such as Lenin and Trotsky. He was influenced by the monistic materialism of Marx. He has great admiration for the age of enlightenment and for the great economists of the seventeenth and the early eighteenth century and for the liberal as well as the socialist thinkers. He considers the utopian element to be characteristic of all forward-looking, romantic and revolutionary thought. He is particularly enamoured of the *humanist materialism* of Feuerbach. He also prefers the scientific naturalism of the eighteenth century to the *dialectical materialism* of Marx which in his view is akin to idealism.

According to Roy, "If the germs of Socialism or Communism grew in the womb of the Capitalist society, then the inspiration for a truly liberating philosophy of the future should also be found in the moral and spiritual values of the so-called bourgeois culture".[4] The communists proudly declare that they have no use for the capitalist culture and bourgeois morality. He believes that the proletariat by itself is not a revolutionary force. He has doubts about the theory of class struggle as propounded by Marx. He said, "The refusal of the contemporary capitalist society to be polarised into two classes according to Marxist prediction throws doubt on the theory of class struggle.... Marxism certainly is wrong as regards the role of the middle class in the capitalist society".[5] He agrees with Lenin that the proletariat have inevitably to be led by the middle class intellectuals organised in a party.

Roy seems to think that even economic factors influence history only when they assume a moral garb. This transformation of the economic factors into moral issues is brought about by thinking individuals. Revolutions are heralded by iconoclastic ideas conceived by gifted individuals. In his thought reason, *romanticism* and revolution co-exist as related concepts, which together characterise man as a creative, forward-looking being. He said, "In the last analysis, there is no contradiction between rationalism and the romantic view of life. The two are harmonised in the idea of revolution".[6]

Nevertheless Roy was categorically opposed to the dictum and the doctrine that the *end* justifies the *means*. To him, it is very doubtful if a moral object can ever be attained by immoral means. In critical moments when larger issues are involved and greater things are at stake, some temporary compromise in behaviour may be permissible. But when practices repugnant to ethical principles and traditional human values are stabilised as the permanent features of the revolutionary regime, the means defeat the end. This is the main reason why communist political practice has not taken the world, not even the working class, anywhere near a new order of freedom and social justice.

Roy does not endorse the Gandhian theory of Trusteeship. He attached the greatest importance to the *individual* and his *liberty*. He wanted a system of government in which the individual citizen would exercise effective control over the people's representatives controlling the machinery of the state. He said, "The defects of formal parliamentary democracy result from the delegation of power. To make *democracy* effective, power must always remain vested in the people, and there must be ways and means for the people to wield the sovereign power effectively not periodically but from day to day".[7] He envisages the formation of local cooperative organisations as the nuclei of a new system of economy. He is convinced of the innate dignity and goodness of man.

REFERENCES

1. M.N. Roy, *Scientific Politics,* Renaissance Publishers, Calcutta, 1947, pp. 36-37.
2. M.N. Roy, *Reason, Romanticism and Revolution,* Vol. II, Renaissance Publishers, Calcutta, 1955, p. 302.
3. *Ibid.*, p. 301.
4. M.N. Roy, *New Humanism,* Renaissance Publishers, Calcutta, 1961, p. 9.
5. *Ibid.*, p. 25.
6. M.N. Roy, *Reason, Romanticism and Revolution,* Vol. I, *op. cit.*, p. 15.
7. M.N. Roy, *New Humanism, op. cit.*, p. 55.

4

TWENTY-TWO THESES

Thesis One

Man is the archetype of society. Co-operative social relationships contribute to develop individual potentialities. But the development of the individual is the measure of social progress. Collectively presupposed the existence of individuals. Except as the sum total of freedom and wellbeing, actually enjoyed by individuals, social liberation and progress are imaginary ideals, which are never attained. Well-being, if it is actual, is enjoyed by individuals. It is wrong to ascribe a collective ego to any form of *community* (viz. nation, class, etc.), as that practice means sacrifice of the individual. Collective well-being is a function of the well-being of individuals.

Thesis Two

Quest for freedom and search for truth constitute the basic urge of human progress. The quest for freedom is the continuation, on a higher level—of intelligence and emotion—of the biological struggle for existence. The search for truth is a corollary thereof. Increasing knowledge of *nature* enables man to be progressively free from the tyranny of natural phenomena, and physical and social environments. Truth is the content of knowledge.

Thesis Three

The purpose of all rational human endeavour, individual as well as collective, is attainment of freedom, in ever-increasing measure. *Freedom* is progressive disappearance of all restrictions on the unfolding of the potentialities of individuals, as human beings, and not as cogs in the wheels of a mechanical social organism. The position of the *individual*, therefore, is the measure of the progressive and liberating significance of any collective effort or social organisation. The success of any collective endeavour is to be measured by the actual benefit for its constituent units.

Thesis Four

Rising out of the background of the law-governed physical nature, the human being is essentially *rational*. Reason being a biological property, it is not the antithesis of will. Intelligence and emotion can be reduced to a common biological denominator. Historical determinism, therefore, does not exclude *freedom* of will. As a matter of fact, human will is the most powerful determining factor. Otherwise, there would be no room for revolutions in a rationally determined process of history. The rational and scientific concept of determinism is not to be confused with the teleological or religious doctrine of predestination.

Thesis Five

The economic interpretation of history is deduced from a wrong interpretation of materialism. It implies dualism, whereas *materialism* is a monistic philosophy. History is a determined process: but these are more than one causative factors. Human will is one of them, and it cannot always be referred directly to any economic incentive.

Thesis Six

Ideation is a physiological process resulting from the

awareness of environment. But once they are formed, ideas exist by themselves, governed by their own laws. The dynamics of ideas run parallel to the process of social *evolution*, the two influencing each other mutually. But in no particular point of the process of the integral human evolution, can a direct causal relation be established between the historical events and the movement of ideas ('ideas' is here used in the common philosophical sense of ideology or system of ideas). Cultural patterns and ethical values are not mere ideological superstructures of established economic relations. They are also historically determined—by the logic of the history of ideas.

Thesis Seven

For creating a new world of freedom, revolution must go beyond an economic reorganisation of society. *Freedom* does not necessarily follow from the capture of political power in the name of the oppressed and exploited classes and abolition of private property in the means of production.

Thesis Eight

Communism or socialism may conceivably by the means for the attainment of the goal of freedom. How far it can serve that purpose, must be judged by experience. A political system and an economic experiment, which subordinate the man of flesh and blood to an imaginary collective ego, be it the nation or a class, cannot possible be the suitable means for the attainment of the goal of *freedom*. On the one hand, it is absurd to argue that negation of freedom will lead to freedom, and, on the other hand, it is not freedom to sacrifice the individual at the altar of an imaginary collective ego. Any social philosophy or scheme of social reconstruction, which does not recognise the sovereignty of the *individual*, and dismisses the ideal of freedom as an empty abstraction, can have no more than a very limited progressive and revolutionary significance.

Thesis Nine

The State being the political organisation of society, its withering away under communism is a utopia which has been exploded by experience. Planned economy on the basis of socialised industries presupposes a powerful political machinery. Democratic control of that *machinery* alone can guarantee freedom under the new order. *Planning* of production for use is possible on the basis of political democracy and individual freedom.

Thesis Ten

State ownership and planned economy do not by themselves end exploitation of labour: nor do they necessarily lead to an equal distribution of wealth. Economic democracy is no more possible in the absence of political democracy than the latter is in the absence of the former.

Thesis Eleven

Dictatorship tends to perpetuate itself. Planned economy under political *dictatorship* disregards individual freedom on the pleas of efficiency, collective effort and social progress. Consequently, a higher form of *democracy* in the socialist society, as it is conceived at present, becomes an impossibility. Dictatorship defeats its professed end.

Thesis Twelve

The defects of formal parliamentary democracy have also been exposed in experience. They result from the delegation of power. To make democracy effective, power must always remain vested in the people, and there must be ways and means for the people to wield the *sovereign* power effectively, not periodically, but from day to day. Atomised individual citizens are powerless for all practical purposes, and most of the time. They have no means to exercise their *sovereignty* and to wield a standing control of the State machinery.

Thesis Thirteen

Liberalism is falsified or parodied under formal parliamentary democracy. The doctrine of *laissez faire* only provides the legal sanction to the exploitation of man by man. The concept of economic man negativates the liberating doctrine of individualism. The economic man is bound to be slave or a slave holder. The vulgar concept must be replaced by the reality of an instinctively rational being who is moral because he is rational. Morality is an appeal to conscience, and conscience is the instinctive awareness of, and reaction to, environment. It is a mechanistic biological function on the level of consciousness. Therefore, it is rational.

Thesis Fourteen

The alternative to parliamentary democracy is not dictatorship; it is *organised democracy*, in the place of the formal democracy of powerless atomised individual citizens. The parliament should be the apex of a pyramidal structure of the State reared on the base of an organised democracy composed of a countrywide network of people's committees. The political organisation of society (the State) will be coincident with the entire society, and consequently the *State* will be under a standing democratic control.

Thesis Fifteen

The function of a revolutionary and liberating social philosophy is to lay emphasis on the basic fact of history that man is the maker of his world—man as a thinking being, and he can be so only as an individual. The brain is a means of production, and produces the most revolutionary *commodity*. Revolutions presuppose iconoclastic ideas. In increasingly large number of men, conscious of their creative power, motivated by the indomitable will to remake the world, moved by the adventure of ideas, and fired with the ideal of a free society of free men, can create the conditions under which democracy will be possible.

Thesis Sixteen

The method and programme of social revolution must be based on a reassertion of the basic principle of social progress. A social renaissance can come only through determined and wide-spread endeavour to educate the people as regards the principles of freedom and rational cooperative living. The people will be organised into effective democratic bodies to build up the socio-political foundation of the post-revolutionary order. *Social revolution* requires in rapidly increasing number, men of new renaissance, and a rapidly expanding system of people's committees: and an organic coordination of both. The programme of revolution will similarly be based on the principle of freedom, reason and social harmony. It will mean elimination of every form of monopoly and vested interest in the regulation of social life.

Thesis Seventeen

Radical democracy presupposes economic reorganisation of society so as to eliminate the possibility of exploitation of man by man. Progressive satisfaction of material necessities is the precondition for the individual members of society unfolding their intellectual and other human potentialities. An economic reorganisation, such as will guarantee a progressively rising standard of living, is the foundation of the radical democratic state. Economic liberation of the masses is an essential condition for their advancing towards the goal of freedom.

Thesis Eighteen

The economy of the new social order will be based on production for use and distribution with reference to human needs. Its political organisation excludes delegation of power, which in practice deprives the people of effective power; it will be based on the direct participation of the entire population through the *People's Committees*. Its culture will be based on universal dissemination of knowledge and on minimum control and maximum scope for, and incentive to, scientific and creative activities. The new society, being founded on reason and science, will necessarily be planned. But it will be planning with the freedom of the individual as its main purpose. The new society will be democratic—politically, economically as well as culturally. Consequently, it will be a democracy which can defend itself.

Thesis Nineteen

The ideal of *democracy* will be attained through the collective efforts of spiritually free men united in the determination of creating a world of freedom. They will function as the guides, friends and philosophers of the people rather than as their would be rulers. Consistently with the goal of freedom, their political practice will be rational and therefore ethical. Their effort will be reinforced by the growth of the people's will to freedom. Ultimately, the radical democratic state will rise with the support of enlightened public opinion as well as intelligent action of the people. Realising that *freedom* is inconsistent with concentration of power, radical democrats will aim at the widest diffusion of power.

Thesis Twenty

In the last analysis, education of the citizens is the condition for such a reorganisation of society as will be conducive to common progress and prosperity without encroaching upon the *freedom* of the individual. The people's committees will be the schools for the political and civic *education* of the citizen. The structure and function of the radical democratic state will enable detached individuals to come to the forefront of public affairs. Manned with such individuals the State *machinery* will cease to be the instrument in the hands of any particular class to coerce others. Only spiritually free individuals in power can smash all chains of slavery and usher in freedom for all.

Thesis Twenty-one

Radicalism integrates science into social organisation and reconciles individuality with collective life; it gives to freedom a moral, intellectual as well as a social content. It offers a comprehensive theory of social progress in which both the dialectics of economic determinism and dynamics of ideas find their due recognition; and it deduces from the same a method and a programme of social revolution in our time.

Thesis Twenty-two

Radicalism starts from the dictum that 'Man is the measure of everything' (Protagoras) or 'Man is the root of mankind' (Marx), and advocates reconstruction of the world as a *commonwealth* and *fraternity* of free men, by the collective endeavour of spiritually emancipated moral men.

5

ROY ON NEW HUMANISM

The new social philosophy according to Roy must start with reviving faith in man regarding his potentialities. Any attempt to promote economic welfare, social reconstruction and political liberty must begin with man. For this reason, he said, humanism was the only alternative not only to communism but to all forms of *institutionalism*. "Democracy can be established only by the reassertion of the humanist tradition. Man is the measure of his world. Being inherently rational he can always learn from experience. He develops his intellectual faculties and moral values in his efforts to secure a better life for himself".[1]

The philosophy of revolution evolved on the basis of the whole stock of human heritage for political action and economic reconstruction is known as 'New Humanism'. It stresses that neither capitalism nor parliamentary system can solve our problems. *Socialism* and *communism* reject the idea of freedom. *New Humanism* is the only alternative which reconciles social organisation and individual freedom. Roy said, "The basic idea of a new revolutionary social philosophy must be that the individual is prior to society, and individual freedom must have priority over social organisation".[2]

The fundamental principles on which New Humanism stands are sovereignty of man and freedom of man. It does not pre-suppose any authority over man. In New Humanism whatever man does is out of his own conviction, out of his own moral sense and without any external force of compulsion. Roy said, "*Radical humanism* envisages a government based on moral sense of the people and therefore everyman's moral sense must be highly developed. Alongwith it, a sense of justice, fairplay and social responsibility must also develop in their fullness".[3] New Humanism is a philosophy to restore supreme confidence in man and requires him not to surrounder even in the deepest gloom. This is a philosophy of positive values.

Roy wanted the Radical Humanist movement to strive for reconstruction of society so as to eliminate all obstacles in the way of progress and development of human personality. It must eliminate production for and unnecessary concentration of control over the means of production. He said, "The endeavour to lay down the humanist foundation of a democratic order must be coordinated with the cooperative reconstruction of the economic life. The result will be creation of a chain of local republics in which *democracy* will be real because it will be direct and economic problems solved on the basis of local resources, with the intelligent initiative and cooperative effort of the citizens".[4]

Man has created society and various political institutions. Even then man is reduced to nothingness. Under the new scheme of humanist revival man is to be restored to his proper place of primacy. Roy said, "Man must be regarded as the archetype of society, because the potentiality of evolving entire social patterns is inherent in every individual. Therefore, he can discharge social responsibilities without a surrounding liberty".[5] New Humanism proclaims the *sovereignty* of man on the authority of modern *science*, which has dispelled all mystery about the essence of man. It maintains that a rational and moral society is possible because man, by nature is rational and therefore can be moral not under any compulsion, but voluntarily, that the sanction of morality is embedded in human nature.

New Humanism aims at a secular, rational morality for opening a new perspective before the world. In it, human dignity, personality, sovereignty and creativeness all acquire meaning. According to Roy, it must be realised that human existence is itself content and *self-sufficient*. Man is capable of working out his destiny and making a better world to live in. The most important feature of humanist philosophy is the belief that there are certain human values which transcend all other considerations, and to develop the human personality is the main purpose of life. All institutions—political, economic and social—must serve the basic purpose of life.

New Humanism rejects economic determinism of Marx and considers human will as the motive force of social evolution. For creating a new world of liberty and social justice, revolution must go beyond mere economic reorganisation of society. It also wants to liberate man from the belief that there is a transcendental source of his humanness. Free from all prejudices, spiritual origin and spiritual slavery, man is allowed freedom to think. Roy said, "A *brotherhood* of men attracted by the adventure of ideas, keenly conscious of the urge for freedom, fired with the vision of a free society of free man and motivated by the will to remake the world, so as to restore the individual in his position of primacy and dignity, will show the way out of the contemporary crisis of modern civilisation".[6]

In the final phase of his life Roy moved away from communism completely and began his journey towards *Radical Humanism*, which according to him is a philosophy of life embracing all aspects of human life. He had discovered the faults and shortcomings of communism. He said, "It is not a question of Western or Indian ways of life. The old Indian way of life was not so good that we should want to preserve it. The western way of life—not because it is western, but because it has led into a blind-alley, is also no attraction. What we need is a new way of life, which is a human way of life, where the qualities of the human being will become decisive and will be allowed to determine the system under which they will work and live".[7]

In this connection it is significant to note that the happenings during and after the Second World War had a big unsettling effect on the over enquiring mind of Roy. It compelled him to re-examine many communist doctrines and theories. V.B. Karniko said, "He found them in communism's utter disregard of and contempt for man. Man, he found, had been reduced to the position of a helpless pawn in the hands of blind economic forces and an insignificant unit in a broad-collectively of a class. That happened also under capitalism and that, according to Roy, was the basic cause of the crisis that had afflicted the world. Neither capitalism nor communism showed the way out of this crisis".[8]

Roy's main contribution to the socio-economic thought is his concept of Humanism. We may call it 'New Humanism' and may compare it with what Mao called *New Man*. Here again the main difference in the approaches of these great thinkers is that while Roy wanted to achieve it through democracy, Mao had the opportunity to try it through a totalitarian state. Das Gupta said, "Twenty-five years ago Roy enunciated *New Humanism* and today Mao wants 'New Man'. How close the conclusions are of Roy and Mao: Nay, their conclusions have coincided in a way. It is indeed striking that the two thinkers have reached the same conclusions of completely remarking 'Man' and yet they have concluded in their own distinct ways—Roy by close study of man and the country's political and social organisations and their workings and it may be noted that he had no opportunity of handling the government machinery by which his theory of all-pervading democracy could be put into operation. But Mao had the unique opportunity of controlling a vast country being the head and dictator of the Government for over two decades".[9]

Roy had seen through long experiences the negative aspects of *capitalism* operating in the form of parliamentary democracy in the political field and the policy of *laissez-faire* in the economic field. The alternative suggested by communism, i.e., dictatorship of the proletariat and central planning were equally bad because instead of liberating man, they made him a slave of the almighty State run by a party dictatorship. He never envisaged this state of affairs when he had the opportunity to work with revolutionary figures like Lenin, Trotsky and Stalin during the earlier part of his revolutionary career. Thus he founded a new movement known as 'Radical Humanism'. It envisaged a new form of political and economic institutions that would guarantee freedom and progress to man as man and not as the member of a nation or a class. He thought of organised democracy and *cooperative economy* as a solution to the crisis which had gripped the world and was dragging it in the direction of war and destruction.

The philosophical foundation of organised *democracy* and cooperative economy is contained in Roy's concept of 'Radical Humanism'. In 1946 he wrote the 'Twenty-Two Theses' which outlined it in the form of categorical statements and the same was elaborated in the form of a manifesto called 'New Humanism' adopted by his Radical Democratic Party in 1947.

The central idea of 'Radical Humanism' is freedom, the supreme value from which all human values are derived. Roy defined freedom as follows: "The function of life is to live. The basic incentive of organic becoming is the struggle for survival. It goes on throughout the long process of biological evolution, until in man it becomes the conscious urge for freedom, the supreme human value. The beginning of man's endless struggle for *freedom* lies in the animal struggle for survival. Everything that man has done, everyone of his acts, cultural progress, scientific achievements, artistic creation—everything has been motivated by that one urge. Man is finite, while the universe is infinite, and his *environment*, in the last analysis, is the whole universe. Consequently, his struggle for freedom is eternal; he can never conquer the universe. Therefore, the urge for freedom is the only eternal thing in the human world".[10]

Further elucidating the philosophy of 'Radical Humanism' Roy contends that as a philosophy of life it covers the entire field of human existence, from abstract thought to social and political reconstruction. Man is the creation of nature, he is an integral part of the physical universe and the universe is a law germed system. Roy said, "Man's being and becoming, his emotions, will, ideas are also predetermined. Therefore, man is essentially rational. The reason in man is an echo of the harmony of the universe".[11]

According to Roy man is moral because he is rational. To put it in other words morality grows as rationality develops. Man created *society* in order to be able to struggle successfully for his existence. He said, "The socialist struggle for human progress, the entire process of human evolution is nothing but the continuation of the struggle for existence on a higher level, where that struggle is no longer guided by instinct and natural selection but by intelligence, choice and reasoning".[12]

Roy conceived the idea of 'Radical Humanism' after having discarded many ideas that he had accepted during the communist phase of his life. He went beyond communism and discovered *Radical Humanism*. It is curious to note that Radical Humanism brought Roy closer to Gandhian thought on many points. Both accepted individual as the central point of all social thought and action. Both stood for decentralisation of political and economic power and both suggested partyless democracy. The fundamental difference between the two lies in the fact that while Roy was a *materialist* and *rationalist*, Gandhiji was a spiritualist. Roy was a constant critic of Gandhiji but during the last two years of his life he became his great admirer due to the simple fact that Gandhiji turned away from power on the attainment of freedom in 1947.

REFERENCES

1. All India Conference of Radical Democratic Party held in Calcutta, December 26 to 30, 1948.
2. M.N. Roy, *Reason, Romanticism and Revolution*, Vol. I, *op. cit.*, p. 284.
3. M.N. Roy, *Quest for Freedom*, *op. cit.*, p. 31.

4. M.N. Roy's speech at the First All India Convention of Radical Humanists, February 4, 1951.
5. M.N. Roy, *Reason, Romanticism and Revolution*, Vol. II, *op. cit.*, p. 287.
6. *Ibid.*, p. 310.
7. M.N. Roy, *Politics, Powers and Parties*, *op. cit.*, p. 167.
8. V.B. Karnaik, *M.N. Roy*, National Book Trust, Delhi, 1980, p. 103.
9. M.N. Roy, *Quest for Freedom*, *op. cit.*, pp. 49-50.
10. M.N. Roy, *New Orientation*, Renaissance Publishers, Calcutta, 1946, p. 23.
11. M.N. Roy, *'Radical Humanism'*, Eastern Economist, Pamphlets, New Delhi, 1952, p. 16.
12. M.N. Roy, *Science and Philosophy*, Renaissance Publishers, Calcutta, 1947, p. 23.

6

ROY ON AGRICULTURE

M.N. Roy was of the opinion that industrial development must be associated with the development of agriculture and agro-based small scale industries. He was fully conscious of the fact that *agriculture* industry and *small-scale industries* are mutually dependent and the development of one sector by implication calls for an integrated development of the other. He said, "A little knowledge of the structure of modern industry shows that even if India would be industrialised to the greatest possible extent within the next ten or fifteen years, not more than perhaps ten million people could be shifted from agriculture to industry. That will be less than a fraction considering the degree of population pressure on the land. That much shift of labour will have no substantial influence in changing the structure of Indian economy, not to mention the standard of living of the Indian people. If it is maintained that the living standard would at least be a little improved by comparison there are other considerations which could be held against that contention. The obvious difficulty will be that, once modern industries are built and begin producing goods on a large scale, India will experience the curious problem of over-production while people continue to suffer from chronic under-consumption. And again, that will be so whether under capitalism or socialism as they are known from contemporary practice".[1]

Roy did not consider that the Russian type of *Socialism* provides an answer to the problems of Indian economy. He said, "If we want to modernise and reorganise Indian economy and increase national wealth, we must naturally begin with the main sector of Indian economy, which is *agriculture*. Again the type of reorganisation of agriculture which is necessary and possible in our country has nothing in common with socialism. The abolition of landlordism is a feature of historically earlier revolutions. And it is yet to be seen whether the abolition of the *Zamindari* system by itself will really have the miraculous effect hoped for".[2]

Unless the land is given to the actual tillers of the soil no progress is possible on the agricultural front. Roy advocates a plan for agricultural *reform*. In his view the ultimate ownership of the land should rest with the State and the peasants should enjoy security and fixity of land tenure on payment of reasonable land revenue to the State. He suggested the setting up of village councils of all the poor and the landless peasants. These Village Councils should be responsible for the redistribution of the land among the landless. He said, "The *peasants* must organise village councils, composed of all the poor and landless peasants, should take charge of the redistribution of the land. The expropriated landlords, village traders, moneylenders and all others owning capital or large property should be excluded from these Village Councils. The reason for such exclusion is plain. It is to protect the interest of the poor peasantry freed from the age-long exploitation of landlordism, and to make the confiscation real".[3]

Roy analysed the nature of *exploitation* of the poor peasantry by the traders. He said, "In the person of the village trader, the agent of the big export firms is to be found in almost every corner of the country. These agents have elaborated a system of taking away by far the greater volume of the produce of the soil in exchange for cheap machine-made commodities, a considerable portion of which consists of domestic necessities and worthless ornaments, thus leaving the *peasant* starving and submerged in debt for the rest of his life.

The crops on the field are sold to the large capitalist concerns before they are harvested or often before they are sown".[4]

Regarding the extent of exploitation of the poor peasantry by the traders, Roy said, "Instances are not rare in which the cultivator is found to be so hopelessly at the mercy of the local dealers or exporters agent, that he has to part with his rice crop from the very field and to go hungry all the year round, or to buy what is left after the choice grains have been exported at a price often several times more than he has received for his crop. And this bad purchase he can make only by mortgaging his landholding or by selling his cattle or plough".[5]

Roy pleads for reorganisation of the rural economy rather than mere *mechanisation*. He said, "Modernisation of *agriculture* is the greatest need of the economic life of our country if production of wealth is to be increased. But this is more a matter of organisation of rural economy than of mechanistry which is widely believed to be the only panacea".[6]

Roy was of the opinion that *modernisation* of agriculture and a reorganisation of the rural economy alone can bring about prosperity through increased production. He said, "The improvement of Indian agriculture presents us with a new problem. Apart from the dogma of nationalism, we have the old theory that in order to increase the productivity of land, agiculture must be mechanised. The plough must be replaced by the tractor and other machinery. But here again we come up against the poverty of the peasants. Few of them can afford a tractor, and to employ machinery profitably, agriculture holdings must be very large. The average holding of the Indian peasants is so small that the application of *machinery* is almost out of question. Therefore, it is argued that existing pattern of agriculture must be abolished in favour of large farms owned by the State, or perhaps formally owned by peasant cooperatives, so that big machinery can be introduced".[7]

If large farms are created and placed in the hands of

private capitalists, it will lead to greater exploitation. So, Roy recommends either State farming or cooperative farming. He said, "Individual cultivation should be replaced by the *large-scale farming* in order to raise the productivity of the soil and utilise modern implements. Only thus can the maximum production be secured by the minimum labour. Large-scale farms, however, become vehicle of intensive exploitation if owned by private capitalists for their own profits. In order that the mass of the peasants should derive advantage from them, these large scale farms should be owned by the state and everybody who works on them should share equally in the produce.... In order to show the peasant the advantage of community ownership, communal agricultural farms should be started to serve as models, under the direct supervision of government experts. Great estates now under a modern system of agriculture and tracts of waste land can be utilised for such communal forms, which will be controlled by the council of peasants who work on them".[8]

Roy maintains for slow and gradual transformation of existing small-scale farming into large-scale cooperative or *collective farms*. This change cannot be brought through legislation but through a process of social education of the masses in favour of such a system. He advocated the abolition of intermediaries and conferring rights on those who actually cultivate it but the final ownership should rest with the state. He also advocated the setting up of large community agricultural farms. He had in mind the idea of collective-cum-cooperative farming for Indian agriculture. He said, "The cultivation of the soil in India, although to a great extent still backward, is being adopted more and more to the exigencies of trade and industry than to the prime necessity of feeding the cultivator and his family. In form, agriculture still remains almost the same as a century ago, but its social character has been modernised".[9].

Roy was of the opinion that the Indian farmers live at the mercy of the village trader. He said, "The position of a village farmer with grains, oilseeds or cotton to sell, but at the same time heavily indebted to the village trader, his only customer, makes the farmer a helpless victim of the latter. Thus this rural trading class is looked upon by both the peasant and the ruined artisan as the cause of their misery. The peasant thinks so because the grip of the trader-usurer is becoming tighter on his throat everyday, while the artisan is deprived of his living by the import of cheap machine-made commodities".[10]

Roy contended that a large mass of rural population is still engaged in rural *handicrafts* simply because they have no other means of livelihood. He said, "There is still to be found a large population in the rural districts engaged in handicrafts, but its economic condition is absolutely helpless. If these unfortunate people are still sticking to the occupations which cannot prevent death from starvation, it is not because they are too fond of these ancestral pursuits to abandon them, but because all other ways of earning their livelihood are blocked".[11]

Roy propounds a new 'Theory of Culture' incorporating the philosophy of hard work, simple living with higher moral values of life. He expresses his preference to moral rather than material advancement of the rural masses. He said, "The function of the tool is to help man earn his subsistence with the minimum effort and time. In modern industry, man can earn a living in return for eight hours work a day. The amount of daily labour could be easily reduced by half. On the contrary, in *handicrafts* man must work twelve hours or more to get the same result. And if a limit is set to the development of tools, he will have no prospect of ever getting out of the drudgery. To attend to one or several fly-shuttles for eight hours a day in a modern factory turns a man into the slave of the machines, but playing the spinning wheel for twelve hours, he becomes a free man, able to soar high spirituality: The change in his mode of occupation would place him on a higher cultural level, although it would lower the standard of his material existence. But that exactly is the desired result. Freed from materialistic temptations, back to simplicity, man would recover his humanness. A remarkable theory of culture—the more man labours, the less he eats, the higher is his moral worth".[12]

Roy propounded a thesis on the nature of the socio-political revolution in India. To quote Grover, "Roy characterised the impending Indian revolution as a bourgeois democratic revolution, which would take the form of clash between a class based on land as the means of production and another based on new means of production, namely, capital. Abolition of non-productive ownership of land is the fundamental feature of social transformation. The only generally beneficial line of economic development opened to India was to carry out an agrarian revolution, and build up modern industry under the control of a really democratic state. That rendered the bourgeois democratic revolution a historical necessity for India".[13]

Roy advocated Village Councils in place of old type of village *Panchayats*. He tried to outline the type of government. He said, "We must set up such a government which will help the poor peasants to buy modern agricultural machinery and improve their primitive agriculture. We will set up Village Councils. Not the old Panchayats over which the village bully ruled. Our councils will be elected by the poor peasants from among themselves and will administer the affairs of the village. The national government will buy modern agricultural implements and place them at the disposal of these village communities which in their turn will rent these out to the peasants at a very moderate charge. As the Village Councils will be controlled by the peasants themselves, the rent will naturally be fixed according to their own capacity to pay. Thus the poverty of the peasant will no longer prevent him from obtaining the help of modern *science* and inventions to free himself from his present misery".[14]

At one stage Roy advocated a strong unitary type of government. He rejected the doctrine of decentralisation of power on the basis of region, language, estate or religion. At a later stage, he pleaded for the recognition of the village as the nucleus and the transformation of the rural society. Grover said, "Roy as a Marxist, stood for a centralised national state, which based on universal suffrage, was the only way to national solidarity. The doctrine of *decentralisation* on the basis of linguistic and communal demarcations was found injurious. He rested his faith on the economic development which destroyed all regional differences and social prejudices. However, Roy laid emphasis on the importance of villages, which should be so constituted as to become basic units of the state. This would save the individual from becoming social atoms. At the same time, Roy was quite clear that a national state could not be built on the foundation of a social organism still greatly dominated by feudal traditions, patriarchal conservation and religious superstitions. Subsequently, Roy moved away from the idea of unitary government".[15]

Roy seems to be in disagreement with the Gandhian approach of *Constructive Programmes* and *Self-help* through the spinning wheel. He said, "We should organise the peasantry. Not by giving them Constructive Programmes, not to teach them Self-help, not to tell them to spin after the hard day's labour in order to earn a few pice more, not to set up dummy arbitration courts without any authority to enforce their own decisions—but to demand the reduction of rents and taxes, to back up such demands by refusing payments and resisting arbitrary collective, to organise mass demonstrations to protest against the imposition of direct taxation such as the salt tax, against high prices, low wages and the payment of usuary. We must learn to direct the organised energy of the rural masses towards the redress of those innumerable grievances which make their lives a burden".[16] He expresses the view that unless the people learnt to asset themselves for the legitimate cause of their socio-economic emancipation, the concept of 'Self-help' loses its effectiveness and relevance.

Roy has built his thesis on the premises that poverty and exploitation is so deep rooted that the same cannot be removed except by changing the entire rural set-up. He expresses the firm opinion that any attempt towards reformist action only help to perpetuate the evil by teaching people to put up with the injustice taking it as the inevitable.

REFERENCES

1. M.N. Roy, *Politics, Powers and Parties*, Renaissance Publishers, Calcutta, 1960, p. 158.
2. *Ibid*., p. 160.
3. M.N. Roy, *India in Transition*, Nachiketan Publishers, Bombay, 1971, p. 265.
4. *Ibid*., p. 50.
5. *Ibid*., p. 52.
6. M.N. Roy, *Politics, Powers and Parties, op. cit*., p. 161.
7. *Ibid*., p. 162.
8. M.N. Roy, *India in Transition, op. cit*., p. 271.
9. *Ibid*., p. 51.
10. *Ibid*., p. 49.
11. *Ibid*., p. 48.
12. M.N. Roy, *India's Message: Fragments of a Prisoner's Diary*, Vol. 2, Renaissance Publishers, Calcutta, 1950, p. 232.
13. D.C. Grover, *M.N. Roy: A Study of Revolution and Reason in Indian Politics*, Minerva Associates, Calcutta, 1973, p. 34.
14. M.N. Roy, *India in Transition, op. cit*., p. 270.
15. D.C. Grover, *M.N. Roy: A Study of Revolution and Reason in Indian Politics, op. cit*., pp. 52-53.
16. M.N. Roy, *India in Transition, op. cit*., pp. 268-69.

7

ROY ON INDUSTRIALISATION

Roy gave serious thought to the importance of industrialisation for India. His main concern seems to be to find a synthesis between modern large-scale industries and the village and small-scale industries based on traditional pattern and organisational structure. In his view *small-scale industries* can also be developed side by side with large-scale industries taking note of their local character.

Roy favour small-scale industries. He had the realisation that highly capital-intensive industries are fraught with the danger of the concentration of economic power in the hands of few capitalists. On one hand he advocates *industrialisation* and on the other hand he is conscious of the risks involved in it. He said, "It is true that India is a poor country. But it is not true that India does not possess enough resources to undertake industrialisation on a useful scale. With the resources she has, a modest beginning can be made, and it is by no means certain that a very high degree of industrialisation would be at all good for India. On the other hand, small-scale industries are of little interest to big capitalists, but they can be started by the people themselves on a local scale".[1]

Roy contends that it would be better to encourage local initiative through state help to set up small-scale industries. He said, "With such measure, much more can be done for immediate economic improvement than by those over-capitalised huge projects which cost too much and must therefore charge too much for their services. In disinterested public workers take the initiative, small-scale projects could easily be undertaken by the local people themselves with relative little help from the government, and that should certainly be forthcoming once a realistic start is made from below".[2]

Modern industries would not solve the problem of *unemployment* for a growing population. The only remedy lies in a total transformation of the Indian economy through a process of a revolution. Roy said, "The poverty of the peasantry has become so chronic and the chances of any radical change so non-existent that a complete agrarian revolution remains as the only solution. Neither to reformed land policy of the government, nor the frankly conservative, if not reactionary programme of the nationalist movement, offers any prospect for betterment. The growth of *large-scale farms* worked by machinery would deprive millions of the hovel; and a step back to *landlordism* would make the progress, with millions of people today living on land as the means of living, retrograde. The population is so vast that it would be impossible for the modern industries, even if they increase to a hundred-fold their present magnitude, to absorb the mass of unemployed, which would come into existence as a result of an extensive introduction of labour-saving machinery in agriculture. Besides the growth of industry would throw into unemployment another large section of the population, the artisans. Thus nothing short of a radical re-adjustment of the national economy can improve the situation. There must be a revolution in order to change not only the superstructure, but the very basis of social economics".[3]

Gandhi's philosophy of socio-economic transformation through Truth, Non-violence, Love and Self-Help did not seem to find conviction with Roy. Roy advocated the application of modern *science* and *technology* in the field of agriculture and industries. He pleaded for adequate state control and initiative to encourage local initiative for small-scale industries. Grover said, "Roy attacks Gandhi's theory of economic welfare, which dwells on simplicity in preference to plenty. It does not mean that socialism is devoid of higher values. On the other hand, material well-being constitutes the basis of intellectual growth and moral development. Man created the machine which socialism proposes to place at the service of man. Gandhism is so much shocked by the machine civilisation that it proposes to throw the baby away with the bath water. *Gandhism* throws back humanity to primitive form of production to enable the people to lead simple life. Roy dismisses *Charkha* as reactionary economics which accounts for Gandhi's failure to come out with an economic programme to win the allegiance of masses, and to make the *Swaraj* intelligible to them".[4]

Roy advocates a process of change whereby labour is shifted to such sphere of production where the productivity of labour is high and conducive to higher national and per capita income. He said, "The method of concentrating on rapid industrialisation by building up heavy industries as a means to raise the standard of living of the people is obviously not suitable to India. The main consideration in favour of this method is that unless labour is shifted from the land to fields of production where the productivity of *labour* is higher, national wealth can't grow; and unless the total national wealth grows and grows quickly, its equitable distribution will not substantially alter the prevailing economic conditions. Before advocating the method of rapid industrialisation we shall have to see if it will produce the desired result".[5]

Roy's support to industrialisation is subject to the condition that it must ensure a higher productivity of labour and a better and more equitable distribution of wealth so as to ensure the solution of the existing economic conditions of the Indian masses. Regarding the role and importance of machinery, he said, "If the metal-using man is culturally more advanced than the savage with the stone-flint, the man of the machine age must be proportionately superior to the artisan of the middle ages. Machine is but the most highly developed tool. It is a part of normal human existence, just as much as the tools of hand industry. You can't advise mankind to discard the machine without declaring by implication, if not in so many words, that the use of tools is incompatible with humanness and animalness; for, in the use of tools is the line of demarcation between animal and man".[6]

Roy opines that unrestricted capitalism is counter-productive to true *democracy*. The labour laws should be supervised by the elected Workers' Council in each factory. There should be a limit on the profits of the capitalists. On one hand he stands for an effective state authority and on the other hand for strong organisations of the workers, artisans and peasants at the grass-root level. He did not advocate a total nationalisation. He said, "If the industries of the country are left entirely as the property of and under the control of the individual capitalist, political *freedom* even under a democratic government will be only a myth. The protection and welfare of the working class therefore demands a certain degree of supervision and restraint over capitalist ownership of industries. The supervision and restraint will be exercised by the Workers' Councils, elected from among and by the workers in the factory. These councils will see that the laws regarding the protection of the workers are enforced and that the profit accruing to the owner does not exceed a certain limit set by the democratic government. In this way the national wealth increased by the development of industries will be as evenly distributed as is possible within the limits of capitalist ownership".[7]

Roy did not favour total *nationalisation* of industries, but private sector functioning under state regulation and control. He believed in industrial development through a state-controlled *private sector* rather than a state-owned *public sector*. He accepted the role of private capital only in the initial stages of industrial growth. He visualised economic planning as an effective tool for the economic reconstruction of India. He not only repudiated private property but advocated a large measure of state control on economic life in conformity with his concept of revolutionary democratic socialism.

REFERENCES

1. M.N. Roy, *Politics, Powers and Parties*, Renaissance Publishers Pvt. Ltd., Calcutta, 1960, p. 159.
2. *Ibid.*, p. 164.
3. M.N. Roy, *India in Transition*, Nachiketa Publishers, Bombay, 1971, pp. 84-85.
4. D.C. Grover, *M.N. Roy: A Study of Revolution and Reason in Indian Politics*, Minerva Associates, Calcutta, 1973, p, 40.
5. M.N. Roy, *Politics, Powers and Parties*, *op. cit.*, p. 157.
6. M.N. Roy, *India's Message: Fragments of a Prisoner's Diary*, Vol. 2, Renaissance Publishers, Calcutta, 1950, p. 231.
7. M.N. Roy, *India in Transition*, *op. cit.*, p. 278.

8

ROY ON POVERTY AND UNEMPLOYMENT

M.N. Roy believed that mere political independence is not enough for the removal of poverty. He believed that *poverty* in India was due to the economic exploitation by the British and also due to India's feudal system. He said, "The poverty of Indian masses is the result of economic exploitation by British *imperialism* and native *feudalism*. The liberation of the Indian masses, therefore, required not only the overthrow of British imperialism but subversion of the feudal-patriarchal order which constituted the social foundations of the foreign practical rule. The corollary was that India needed a social revolution, not mere national independence".[1]

Roy considers Industrial backwardness as the root cause of India's *poverty* and so he recommends rapid industrialisation through the use of modern science and technology as the only solution. He admits that industrial development can take place through the capitalist system of private enterprise and mode of production.

Political power and the form of government is a precondition to achieve the same desired goal, though through different means. Roy said, "Although there are two methods advocated, and hotly disputed, for improving the economic conditions in a backward country, both postulate rapid industrialisation through the application of modern *science* and *technology* to the process of production. Both maintain that the cause of India's poverty is her industrial backwardness, and unless modern industries are built up in the shortest time, the standard of living in India can't be raised. One of the methods advocated for the purpose is the old capitalist mode of production, leaving it so private initiative and capital to bring about the desired state of affairs. As against this, there is the point of view pressed by various shades of socialist and communist opinion. These two latter have difference as ragards the policies and methods of coming to power, which is a precondition postulated by all, but their economic programmes are essentially the same".[2]

Regarding the economic and social disparities among the different sections of the Indian population, Roy attributed it to lack of opportunity rather than lack of ability. He contends that inequalities in the field of education and culture are also due to this lack of opportunity. He said, "It is not natural inferiority but economic disability that creates such a wide gulf between the rich privileged classes and the poor and downtrodden masses. The wages they receive are not sufficient to feed their children; how then can they send them to school, especially in a country where education is neither free nor compulsory? No, it is not natural inferiority; they are maintained in poverty so that the few may live in luxury".[3]

Roy contends that poverty is the result of exploitation because the labour does not get the full reward for his work. He said, "The people who have paid for the house are said to own it, though they have done nothing to bring it into existence. They have not laid one brick; they have not moved a piece of stone; they have not carried one pitcher of water. Yet we are told: The owners have paid the workers wages for their labour. Where did the owner get this money with which they paid wages to the workers? They did not coin it, neither did it drop from heaven. This money with which the workers are paid their wages does not belong to the owners, because it has been gained by *exploitation*, by robbing other workers of the fruits of their *labour*. The money has been gained from profits made on land or industry or trade and all profits, as we have seen, are made from the unpaid labour of the working class. Thus the wealth of the rich does not rightfully belong to them but to those who have worked to produce it".[4]

During the last phase of life Roy came closer to the Gandhian point of view. Regarding the poverty of the Indian rural population he has rightly attributed it to the low level of agricultural productivity. He contends that mere passing of *legislation* cannot solve the problem unless traditional methods of cultivation are changed and the entire rural economic structure is transformed through modern scientific techniques. He said, "The main cause of the *poverty* of our peasantry is the low level of agricultural productivity due to the fragmentation of land into uneconomic holdings and the absence of an active urge on the part of the peasants to improve their position by greater effort and enterprise. Such a problem, which has its root deep in the social soil of the country, can't be solved by merely passing laws. The primary and perhaps the only condition for improving the condition of the peasantry is to change the methods of production and of rural economy as a whole".[5]

Roy contends that people should fight hard against the existing system of injustice and exploitation in every sphere of India's socio-political and economic life. He said, "Our object should be to create discontent everywhere against the present system of *exploitation*, and to intensify it wherever it exists. Thus the ideal of *Swaraj* will be brought within the understanding of the workers and peasants of India. Let us lead them forward under the slogans: Down with Foreign Rule, Down with all Exploitation, Land to the Peasant and Bread to the Worker".[6]

Roy is emphatic on the need of educating the masses. Religious *superstitions* and fatalistic beliefs make the poor people believe that if fate has made them poor they should remain contented with it. He wanted this belief to be removed through mass education. He said, "We must educate the ignorant workers. We must show them how they are robbed and exploited. Many do not know what slaves they are; they think it a virtue to be poor. We must teach them that those who preach the virtues of poverty are not true spiritual guides, but the protectors of the interests of the master class".[7]

Roy pleads for a total change of the existing socio-economic relations through a sort of evolution to be brought about by mass movement. Real freedom, social justice, economic progress and prosperity can be achieved only by bringing about radical changes in the basic structure of the Indian society and its economic institutions. He suggested some measures of socio-economic reform. D.C. Grover said, "The revolutionisation of the established social relations is a condition for real national freedom, progress and prosperity. This leads Roy to advocate nationalisation of railways, mines, waterways, telegraphs, etc. Development of modern industries with state aid, protective labour legislation with recognition of unions and right to strike, workers councils in industries, profit sharing in all big industries, free and compulsory education, separation of state and religion, full social, economic and political rights for women, are included by Roy in the programme of Jacobinist reconstruction".[8]

Roy regarded *poverty* as the real issue in India. Rapid industrial development and increase in agricultural productivity through the use of modern and scientific techniques of production alone can solve the basic problem of poverty. Change in the outlook of the people through mass education can secure a greater involvement of the masses in the task of securing political *freedom* and economic *reconstruction* and development by creating in them a sort of consciousness and better realisation of their rights and obligations.

The problem of industrial *unemployment* was not the dominant issue in Roy's time. The only problem that existed was that of unemployment among the rural population. In India, unemployment was the outcome of the decay of the centuries old *small-scale industries* and crafts. Decline of the native industries had a direct bearing on rural unemployment in India. *Agriculture* alone could not provide employment to the growing rural population. He regards the huge unemployed mass of rural population as a deadweight on the rural economy of India. He said, "The huge mass of agricultural workers is a deadweight on the rural population of India. It came into existence not by the process of the economic evolution of society as in the European countries; it was created by the destruction of the native craft industries, which till the earlier decades of the 19th century employed 25 per cent of the entire population of the country".[9]

Roy contends that agriculture cannot provide full time regular employment to the entire rural population throughout the year. He also contends that the possibility of rural unemployment getting work as hired labour on agricultural farms is scarce for the simple reason that bulk of the agricultural operations are carried on by small and marginal farmers. He said, "At least six months in the year they are without work or are employed very irregularly. Since nearly two-third of the entire cropped area of the country is cultivated by small farmers holding on an average 8 acres per family of six (at the minimum) and since distribution of the greater part of the remaining one-third (about, 100,000,000 acres out of 106,000,000) is also so subdivided as to preclude the employment of any considerable number of hired labourers, the possibility of this large mass of field workers being absorbed into the agricultural industry is very limited".[10] He recommends rapid industrialisation, modernisation of agriculture and creation of large agricultural farms under state ownership to solve the problem of unemployment.

Roy regarded unemployment as a twin problem of poverty. He believed that agriculture alone could not provide full time regular employment to rural masses even as hired labour. Besides rapid industrialisation and modern agricultural methods, rural industries should be established to reduce the pressure of population on land. He was conscious of the fact that agriculture, industry and small-scale industries are mutually dependent on one another for economic growth and a solution of the problem of poverty and unemployment.

REFERENCES

1. *M.N. Roy's Memoirs*, Allied Publishers, Delhi, 1964, p. 76.
2. M.N. Roy, *Politics, Powers and Parties*, Renaissance Publishers, Calcutta, 1960, p. 156.
3. M.N. Roy, *India in Transition*, Nachiketa Publications, Bombay, 1971, p. 280.
4. *Ibid.*, p. 279.
5. M.N. Roy, *Politics, Powers and Parties, op. cit.*, p. 161.
6. M.N. Roy, *India in Transition, op. cit.*, p. 284.
7. *Ibid.*, p. 281.
8. D.C. Grover, *M.N. Roy: A Study of Revolution and Reason in Indian Politics*, The Minerva Associates, Calcutta, 1973, p. 52.
9. M.N. Roy, *India in Transition, op. cit.*, p. 55.
10. *Ibid.*, p. 56.

9

ROY ON SOCIETY

M.N. Roy laid great emphasis on individual dignity, initiative and liberty. He gave the central place to the individual in his political philosophy and criticised the political, economic and social systems. To him, individual was an end and all other associations and organisations were means. The individual was sovereign and source of all powers. Man was moral and good by nature. He tried to influence the spirit of self-reliance in the *individual*. He was the champion of individual freedom. Freedom was an essential aspect of human nature and the basic human value. His entire philosophy was concerned with satisfying the man's urge for *freedom*. Without freedom, man was not a human being in real sense.

Roy was a staunch individualist. He did not accept any authority over the individual. Individual was a biological entity to him. He laid emphasis on the unfoldment of the individual. He believed in man's ability and desire. His approach to the individual was rational. His Humanism excludes supernaturalism and affirms that man with, his increasing power over nature is maker of his future.

Roy criticised the *totalitarian* State of Soviet Russia. He advocates the diffusion of power to the lowest level. He was in favour of giving the least responsibilities to the State. He criticised the nation State and his ideal was a World State. He gave a full account of the origin of the State and its distinction. He believed that in the organised democracy, the State will be coincident with the entire society and consequently will be under a standing democratic control.

In the early phase of Roy's political life, he was inclined towards Marxian theory of revolution, that is, class struggle and *proletarian* revolution, and violent means to achieve the objective of revolution. In his later phase, he criticised and abandoned the Marxian theory and the technique of violent *revolution*. To him, revolution meant an all-round change in all aspect of man as well as his institutions. He favoured gradual replacement of the old order by the new social order to bring about a social revolution. *Revolution* was a long term process of social change and not an event. He regarded revolution as a means and not as end in itself. He criticised the various violent revolutions of the world. He advocated revolution by consent. To him, philosophical revolution was a precondition for a successful democratic revolution in India.

Man is the centre of Roy's philosophy. He holds the view that individual is the end and other political and social institutions are means to this end. To him, individual has created the *society* and the State and he is prior to these institutions. He said, "We find that society is the creation of individuals. The individual comes first; he is prior to society; society is for attaining the end, which is the freedom and progress of the individual".[1] He believed in the sovereignty of the people.

Roy criticised all the existing socio-political philosophies. According to him, the crisis of modern civilisation is spiritual crisis. He holds that man is a physical entity. His approach to understand human nature is biological. Human nature is subject to the evolutionary process. There is a continuity of progress from the sub-human level to the human level. He said, "The struggle for existence in the negative sense is quest for freedom. The environments are continually trying to crush the organism, and the struggle for existence is the striving of the organism to free itself from the tyranny of nature. On the sub-human biological level, that is very largely mechanical struggle. But the quest for freedom is purposive. When the struggle for existence takes place with purposiveness on the human level of evolution, we call it quest for freedom".[2]

Reason, morality and *freedom* are the triple eternal attributes of *human nature*. Rationality is a biological property in man. He held that the intellectual and spiritual life of man was conditioned by the elementary instinct of reason, which was a product of pre-human biological evolution. So, rationality is a biological function. He holds that superstition, magic, fetishism, animism and natural religion can be traced to the instinctive rationality of primitive man.

According to Roy, morality can be traced to man's inmate rationality. There is a causal relation between rationality and *morality*. He said, "In the light of modern scientific knowledge, it is discovered that man's rationality is a biological property. Reason is not a metaphysical category. Moral values are placed on a firm foundation when they are referred back to innate rationality of man. They need no other sanction than conscience, which is not the voice of God, but results from rationality. The discovery of physical basis of reason and the rationalist secular sanction of morality free Humanism from the mystic connotation traditionally associated with it".[3]

Man chooses good from bad instinctively which is a biological property, not by any inner voice. Roy said, "There are rules of conduct even among higher animals. These rules go into the composition of human instincts. They are part of man's biological heritage—the constant of *human nature*. In man, they express themselves as the sense of morality. He knows from experience what is good for him and what is bad for him. Therefore, he generalises what is good for him, is good for all like himself, and what is bad for him is also bad for all. That is the origin of morality".[4]

Freedom is an essential aspect of human nature. There is no contradiction between the reason and freedom. Roy said, "Raising out of the background of the law-governed physical nature, the human nature is essentially *rational*. Reason, being a biological property, it is not the anti-thesis of will. Intelligence and emotion can be reduced to a common biological denominator. Historical determinism, therefore, does not exclude freedom of the will".[5] To him, the rational and moral individual is the end, and the social and political institutions are the means. These institutions must help the individual to realise his fullest freedom.

Roy defined the term *freedom*. He said, "Freedom is progressive disappearance of all restrictions on the upholding of the potentialities of individuals, as human beings, and not as cogs in the wheels of a mechanised social organism".[6] Again he said, "Quest for freedom in human evolution is purposive. The struggle for existence is no longer carried out by mechanical adoption on the human level, it is carried on by purposive efforts for the conquest of nature. Science is a search for truth and it is the result of man's quest for freedom. Therefore, we say that search for truth is the corollary to the search for freedom".[7]

Roy regarded freedom as the basic human value. He did not equate it with national independence nor with the ending of the *exploitation* of the masses. He believed that free individuals can alone build up a society of freedom and *equality*. He was not satisfied with physical freedom only. He placed the *intellectual freedom* at the top in his structure of freedom. He was not in favour of giving unlimited freedom to the individual. Man should not be motivated by evil objectives for personal gains only.

Roy criticised *liberalism, socialism, fascism, nazism, nationalism*, etc. He said, "Nation is a metaphysical concept, yet, human beings, of flesh and blood, must sacrifice everything to make the nation great and glorious. That is the essence of Nationalism. That is, to sacrifice, a reality at the altar of a fiction, of an illusion".[8] According to him, nationalism is a medieval idea. It maintains that nation is more important than the individuals who compose it.

Roy rejected the idea of *God* and *religion*. He said, "I

deduce my conclusions not from books but from experience.... Ever since my boyhood I have fought against injustice and for freedom. When I realised that God presented the greatest obstacles on the path of human freedom, I rejected God and since then, I have fought against those who claim to derive their authority from God".[9]

Roy regarded freedom as the supreme value which was the source of other human values. He said, "However, I regard freedom as the supreme value, from which all human values are derived. *Freedom* is the supreme value because the urge for freedom is the essence of human existence; and it is never in the danger of being mystified because it can be traced all the way down the progress of biological evolution; indeed it is coincident, if not actually identical, with life. Since all the ethical values are derived from the soulless, animal heritage of man, they need no sanction, which transcends human existence".[10]

Roy laid emphasis on *individual freedom*. He believed that only individual could experience freedom. He believed that freedom was not an instrumental value. Culture is the foundation of freedom. He, who feels completely in harmony with his cultural background, should feel himself to be free. He said, "Economic well-being and political freedom are also ingredients of the total human culture.... But in the last analysis, greater emphasis should be laid on the deeper layers of human nature. Freedom does not concern merely the relations between man and man. In the first place, it must be experienced individually. Keenly conscious of the urge for freedom and capable of experiencing it, individuals will build a really free *society*. *Culture*, therefore, is the foundation of freedom, which can be reinforced by the satisfaction of all other human requirements".[11]

Roy believed that freedom could not be realised by immoral means. He said, "Quest for freedom, knowledge, truth—that is the hierarchy of humanist axiology. Our values are not autonomous dieties; they are inter-related, locally as well as antologically. Therefore, we say that freedom cannot be attained by immoral means, nor will an enlightened man be a liar".[12] Man can be more free if he is more independent economically. For the moral and intellectual freedom, economic independence is necessary. He said, "Progressive satisfaction of material necessities is the precondition for individual members of society unfolding their intellectual and other finer human potentialities. An economic reorganisation, such as will guarantee a progressively rising standard of living, is the foundation of the Radical Democratic State. Economic liberation of the masses is an essential condition for their advancing towards the goal of freedom".[13] He criticised every system which attacked the individual and his liberty. The social institutions were made by men to exercise their freedom. He was a great advocate of individual's dignity and his liberty.

Roy believed that any institution was not above the individual. Every institution had been created by the individuals for their benefit. Society was the sum total of individuals. The society and the State were artificial structure created by men. He said, "Coming out of the background of biological evolution the human species starts their struggle as individuals. In the course of time, the isolated individuals realised that together they could carry on the struggle more successfully. That was the origin of society".[14] Further he said, "Primitive men created society for the purpose of carrying on the business of regulating their affairs and relations. In the beginning, the purpose was mainly to defend themselves against the impact of natural phenomenon and more powerful beasts, and, later on, to march ahead on the road to human progress on higher levels. Subsequently, when the original human communities became larger, an increasingly electorate machinery had to be created for carrying on public administration of society which came to be known as State".[15]

Regarding the role of the State, Roy was influenced by the Marxian-Leninist interpretation of the State in his earlier phase of political life. According to him, the functions and responsibilities of the State would be limited so that it could not encroach upon the freedom of the individual. The ideal of *Stateless society* is obviously an absurd utopia. He said, "It was completely forgotten that form the primitive time society was formed, all institutions had been created by man like so many instruments to serve the purpose of his being and becoming. Ultimately, it came to be believed that the creation was of greater importance than the creator, to the extent it was entitled to claim the creator of its first victim".[16]

State would be limited by the objective of the freedom of the individual. Roy said, "Today, the State has become an abstraction. In the written Constitutions, the State is divided in three branches the legislative, the executive and the judiciary. If that is all that the State is, then the States must exist only in the capitals and nowhere else. The State, supposed to be the political organisation of society as a whole, has come to be completely divorced from the life of society, if you think of society in terms of human beings constituting society. the individual has nothing to do with the State, the political administration of society. It exists only in some central place, far away, beyond the reach and influence of the members of society, and from there makes decisions and imposes its decisions and the people have no say in them".[17]

According to Roy, the State should create conducive conditions for *individual freedom*. It should maintain harmony in social relations and coordinate the functions of different autonomous institutions. He made a distinction between the State and the government. The State is a political organisation of a country, and the government is to administer its affairs. He said, "The first thing that must be known is that the State and the Government are not the same thing. The function of the Government is to administer the affairs of a State. The Government is composed of a number of individuals, some of whom may change from time to time, and others act as permanent officials".[18] He criticised the ideas of Nationalism.

His ideal was World State. He visualised a *Cosmopolitan* commonwealth of freemen and women.

Roy believed in *terrorism* during his early phase of his political career. He placed his faith in Marxian theory of revolution and abandoned his old idea of terrorism. He said, "An important historical event which marks the close of a given historical period and opens up a new one is called a revolution. Since the social factors, economic classes and political institutions, that used to be benefited by the state of affairs obtaining in the closing period, would not permit a change which spells the end of their domination, often their total annihilation, without a fierce resistance, political violence and social convulsion are usually the features of the historical phenomena which is called revolution. The forces that go into the making of the new epoch are originally conceived and go on gathering strength within the framework of the old which eventually must burst if the germs of the new contained therein are to fully fructify. This process is to be noticed throughout all the physical existence. Revolution, therefore, is in the very nature of things; it is quite constitutional".[19]

According to Roy, the process of history is obstructed by the constraints of the society, which puts a limit to human creativeness, mental as well as physical. He remarked, "The urge for progress and freedom, born out of the biological struggle for existence, asserts itself with a renewed vigour to break down the obstacle. A new social order conducive to a less hampered unfolding of human potentialities is visualised by men, embodying the liberating ideas and cultural values created in the past. A new philosophy is born out of the spiritual heritage of mankind, to herald a reorganisation of society".[20]

Roy rejected the Marxist theory of revolution in his humanist phase. He said, "Then we discovered what is called a new way of Revolution. Gradually by a process of critical thinking, we were led to doubt the very notion of Revolution, which maintains that history is not a continuous process, but that there must be breaks. We re-examined that generally accepted theory of history, which we ourselves had accepted for many years, subjected it to the search light of history. History has not been marked by periods of cataclysms. There has been a ziz-zag, upward and downward movements, but nowhere there has been such a thing that an entire old order had been abolished and something entirely new come into its place".[21] In this phase of his political life, he stood for 'Revolution by consent'. He rejected the theory of class-struggle.

In his humanist phase, Roy preferred philosophical revolution through peaceful means. He said, "The cataclysmic way of revolution is not the only way of revolution, that way has compelled us too often to use those bad means that do not lead to good ends".[22] According to him, behind every institution there were men and ideas and unless these were changed there could be no social reconstruction. Revolution was a means to an end, not end in itself. The Marxian theory of revolution and the Russian revolution were negation of freedom. To him, Russian revolution was neither according to Marxian schedule nor was a proletarian revolution. It was also not a means to freedom.

To establish a good society, the individuals should be made good through the instrumentality of *education*. He advocated philosophical revolution to bring about awareness in the society. He said, "Revolutions are heralded by iconoclastic ideas conceived by gifted individuals. A brotherhood of men attracted by the adventures of ideas, keenly conscious of the urge for freedom, fired with the vision of a free society of free men and motivated by the will to remake the world".[23] All the people should be included in the revolutionary forces. He remarked, "Revolutions presuppose iconoclastic ideas. An increasingly large number of men conscious of their creative power, motivated by the indomitable will to remake the world, moved by the adventure of ideas, and fired with the ideal of a free society of freemen, can create the conditions under which democracy will be possible".[24] The immediate aim of the revolution was to educate the people not to change the institutions.

Roy suggested the method of *education* and persuasion for social change. He favoured gradual replacement of the old by the new social order. He suggested that the propagators of new philosophy would organise the study clubs to create a democratic atmosphere in society. He said, "After all people in a small place can organise their own schools their producers and consumers cooperatives. They can take the initiative in digging wells, building roads, improving public sanitation, etc. They can do it here and now, without waiting, either for government to do it, or for revolution to happen".[25] The study clubs would be converted into people's committees and thus parliamentary democracy might be finally converted into Radical democracy and the party Government into a People's Government.

REFERENCES

1. M.N. Roy and Philip Spratt, *Beyond Communism*, Renaissance Publishers, Calcutta, 1947, p. 116.
2. V.N. Ojha, *M.N. Roy and his Philosophical Ideas*, Shankhand Prakashan, Muzaffarpur, 1969, p. 233.
3. M.N. Roy, *Reason, Romanticism and Revolution*, Vol. I, Renaissance Publishers, Calcutta, 1952, Preface, p. vi.
4. *Ibid.*, p. 143.
5. M.N. Roy and Philip Spratt, *Beyond Communism*, *op. cit.*, p. 143.
6. *Ibid.*, p. 142.
7. V.N. Ojha, *M.N. Roy and his Philosophical Ideas*, *op. cit.*, p. 312.
8. *Ibid.*, p. 205.
9. K.C. Jena, *Contributions of M.N. Roy to Political Philosophy*, S. Chand and Company, New Delhi, 1968, pp. 15-16.
10. M.N. Roy, *Politics, Power and Parties*, Renaissance Publishers, Calcutta, 1960, pp. 10-11.
11. *The Radical Humanist*, Vol. 40, 4-7-1976, p. 3.
12. M.N. Roy, *Politics, Power and Parties*, *op. cit.*, p. 12.
13. M.N. Roy and Philip Spratt, *Beyond Communism*, *op. cit.*, p. 149.

14. M.N. Roy, *Reason, Romanticism and Revolution*, Vol. II, *op. cit.*, p. 283.
15. *The Radical Humanist*, 25-1-1956, p. 36.
16. M.N. Roy, *Reason, Romanticism and Revolution*, Vol. II, *op. cit.*, pp. 268-69.
17. M.N. Roy, *Politics, Power and Parties*, *op. cit.*, p. 61.
18. M.N. Roy, *Independent India*, Vol. IV, No. 7, 18-2-1940, p. 7[illegible].
19. G.A. Adhikari, *Documents of the History of the Communist Party of India*, Vol. II, Peoples Publishing House, New Delhi, 1974, p. 442.
20. M.N. Roy, *Reason, Romanticism and Revolution*, Vol. I, *op. cit.*, p. 14.
21. *The Radical Humanist*, 8-9-1957, p. 447.
22. *Ibid.*
23. M.N. Roy, *Reason, Romanticism and Revolution*, Vol. II, *op. cit.*, p. 310.
24. M.N. Roy and Philip Spratt, *Beyond Communism*, *op. cit.*, p. 148.
25. *The Radical Humanist*, 26-8-1956, p. 403.

10

ROY ON SOCIALISM

M.N. Roy changed some of his ideas from time to time in the light of experience. He was an ardent Marxist in his early phase of political career. He began by analysing the Indian society from the Marxian view point. He came to the conclusion that the reason of poverty of the Indian masses was not merely the foreign economic exploitation but Indian bourgeois class also played important role in exploiting the natives. He believed in *scientific socialism* and its evolutionary nature. *Socialism* was the common ownership of the means of production and distribution and equal opportunities to all the people. In the beginning he agreed to bring socialism by the power of the State.

Roy was not satisfied with *Gandhism* and the bourgeois programme of the Indian National Congress. He laid great emphais on agricultural development of the country. He suggested cooperative farming. To balance the economy of the country he favoured setting up of *industries*. An agro-industrial economy was prescribed by him as the remedy for India and its development. He gave a lot of importance to planning in the economic development.

Roy renounced Marxism in his later stage. He came to the conclusion that *Marxian socialism* was not the solution for the problems of humanity in general and India in particular. He grew into vehement critiques of the Russian *totalitarianism* and *Statism*. His ideologies and thought went beyond Communism. He developed the philosophy of *Radical*

Humanism in the post-independence period.

Roy agreed that the main problem was not that of production but of *centralisation*. He advocated the maximum *decentralisation*. He proposed to reorganise the political and economic system independent of the State interference. He visualised the pyramidal structure of the political and economic system. He agreed on cooperative agriculture.

Roy took active part in the mobilisation of the World Communist movement as an official of the Communist International. He was the most colourful of all non-Russian Communists in the era of Lenin and Stalin. He did not like orthodox nationalism. He did not like *democratic socialism*. He believed that every possible human needs should be satisfied. He believed in the enrichment of the individuals.

Roy was a staunch Marxist in the second phase of his political life. He gave a Marxist interpretation to the modern Indian history. To him, India was not under the feudal system. The feudal system was destroyed by peaceful means. According to Roy, India was divided into four distinct classes, namely (i) the landed aristocracy, including the native chiefs, (ii) the bourgeoisie and the intellectuals, (iii) the petty peasantry, and (iv) the working class, including the landless peasants.

The Indian peasantry was subjected to the *exploitation* of foreign as well as native capital. Roy said, "The secret of misery of the rural population lies in the fact that the agricultural production has been brought completely within the sphere of capitalist exploitation, foreign and native combined. The unrestricted export of foodgrains, together with the merciless speculation carried on by the native the native traders, raises the price continually on the one-hand, while, on the other, the lack of *employment* among an ever-growing section of the rural population creates great scarcity of money. So, even when there is food, the people die of hunger, because they have no money to buy it".[1]

Proletariat was the class of industrial workers living

exclusively on wages earned in the cities in India. According to Roy, the development of large-scale industry would determine the future of India. It would strengthen the labourers. Socialism was more than a philosophy of struggle and reconstruction. It was a revolutionary philosophy of life. To quote A.K. Hindi, "Socialism is not equalitarianism. It does not seek to level down humanity to a uniform standard. *Socialism* will establish equality only in respect of opportunity. In the socialist society, every man and woman will have equal opportunity to attain the highest level of creativeness and intellectual progress. Artificially created inequalities will be removed".[2]

Roy made a distinction between *Marxism* and *Communism*. To him, Marxism was a philosophy and Communism was only a political strategy. He said, "In brief, socialism is the abolition of private property in the means of production, distribution and exchange. The basic thing, however, is production. Private property in that key position of public economy once abolished, socialisation of distribution and exchange inevitably follows. Therefore, the more exact definition of socialism would be abolition of private property in the means of production".[3]

A programme for the Indian National Congress was prepared and circulated on the eve of Gaya Congress held in December 1922. It advocated complete national independence for India, universal suffrage and a federal republic. Its social and economic programme contained the following items:

(a) Abolition of landlordism,
(b) Reduction of land rent to a minimum,
(c) State aid for modernisation of agriculture,
(d) Abolition of all indirect taxes and a progressive income tax,
(e) Nationalisation of public utilities,
(f) Development of modern industries under State aid,
(g) Eight hour day. Fixation of minimum wages by

legislation,

(h) Legalisation of labour organisations,
(i) Worker's Councils in big industries,
(j) Profit sharing to be introduced in all big industries,
(k) Free and compulsory education,
(l) Separation of State and religion,
(m) A national militia to replace the standing army.[4]

In 1926, Roy emphasised the importance of a People's Party in his book, *The Future of Indian Politics*. He criticised the Swaraj Party as a defender of capitalism and landlordism. In December 1929, at Lahore, the Indian National Congress accepted the complete national independence resolution as its immediate objective. Roy welcomed the decision and put before the Congressmen a concrete programme of national revolution through his pamphlet, *The Lessons of the Lahore Congress*. It included the following items:

"(a) Establishment of a Federal Republic of India with an advanced Democratic Constitution, the Executive being fully responsible to a single chamber Parliament elected by universal (men and women) adult suffrage,
(b) Provincial autonomy in local matters, the province, reconstructed for assuring as far as possible linguistic and religious homogeneity, having Government as democratic as the Central Government,
(c) Abolition (without compensation) of the Native States and landlordism by the degree of the Democratic National States empowering the peasants to confiscate the land,
(d) Nationalisation of the land, the cultivators having the occupancy right in return for the payment to the Government of a unitary land-tax, which shall not exceed 15 per cent of the net income,

(e) Abolition of all other charges on the peasantry (for example irrigation-tax) and of indirect taxation (salt-tax, excise duties, protective customs duty, etc.),
(f) Complete exemption of taxation for peasants living on uneconomic holdings,
(g) Liquidation of agricultural indebtedness in the case of the peasants in the state of insolvency,
(h) Legislation for the control of usury (interest not to exceed 10 per cent per annum),
(i) Organisation of agricultural banks with State aid for providing cheap credit to the peasants,
(j) Nationalisation of the mineral resources and public utilities,
(k) Legislation fixing the working day for the wage-labourer to eight hours,
(l) Minimum wages guaranteeing a constantly rising standard of living of the worker to be fixed by law,
(m) Social insurance against unemployment, sickness, old age and maternity, the employers and the contributing 75 per cent of the fund,
(n) Legislation of Trade Unions and the worker's right to strike and organise their class political party,
(o) Freedom of the press, platform and association,
(p) Freedom of religion and worship,
(q) Protection for minorities,
(r) Right to bear arms
(s) Free and compulsory primary education".[5]

Roy was put in jail for six years (1931-36). During his jail period, he modified some of the formulations of Marxism. To quote L.P. Sinha, "During this period of forced seclusion he pondered over some of the assumptions of Marxism and started modifying some of them, specially those in respect of the strategy and tactics of revolution. He came gradually to occupy a Menshevik position, and held that the existing stage in Indian *Revolution* was only one of Bourgeois Democratic Revolution. Though he did not deny the possibility of National

Revolution passing over into a socialist revolution in a hypothetical future, yet for all practical purposes he argued as if this would not happen".[6]

Roy rejected the Marxian principle—the dictatorship of the proletariat as the necessary means to achieve socialism. In India, the proletariat was numerically weak and politically inexperienced. According to Roy, bourgeois democratic revolution was a historical necessity for India. To Roy, the only way for the economic development of India was to carry out an agrarian revolution, and build up modern industry under the control of a really democratic State. He said, "The introduction of the mechanical means of *production* on a large scale, the abolition of all precapitalist restriction on production, the attainment of a certain minimum economic level"[7] were the historic preconditions for the establishment of socialism. In his opinion, political freedom for India was the first postulate for the ultimate objective of socialist society. He remarked that the political independence of the nation would be followed by the economic emancipation of the masses.

Roy organised the Radical Democratic Party in December 1940. He advocated Twentieth Century Jacobinism. He was of the opinion that Marxism could not be applied on our then existing problems. To him, Marxism applied to a bourgeois democratic revolution, Marxist theory applied in practice to the problems of the bourgeois democratic revolution, is Jacobinism. Therefore, Marxism applied to the social problems of the seventeenth and eighteenth century, can be called twentieth century Jacobinism. He considered twentieth century Jacobinism as something midway between a bourgeois revolution and a proletarian revolution. He said, "Once the revolution takes place in our time, though with a Jacobin ideology and with a Jacobinist programme, the tendency towards a direct development to socialism, which was inherent in Jacobinism, will most probably prevail in our country".[8]

Roy formulated a scheme for *planning* in India, namely, *Peoples' plan*. In May 1944, the Radical Democratic Party adopted the Peoples' plan. He laid down three conditions for the economic development of any country. They were (1) abundance of labour, (2) availability of capital to be invested and (3) internal market. The salient features of the Peoples' plan were the following:

(1) The primary motive of production will be to supply the requirements of the people to raise the standard of living as distinct from increasing purchasing power;
(2) Priority for the agricultural production through the mechanisation, modernisation and collectivisation;
(3) Expansion of agricultural production coupled with rationalisation of agricultural economy, would relieve the burden on the peasantry by nationalising land and liquidating indebtedness;
(4) Expansion of present industries and establishments of new ones for supplying the minimum requirements of the people, which are not at present satisfied;
(5) State financing of the mechanisation of agriculture and expansion of industries for supplying the requirements of the people;
(6) Requirements to be satisfied are food, shelter, clothing, health and education;
(7) State control of industries financial with public funds;
(8) The per cent control of industries financial with public funds;
(9) To relieve the pressure of labour on land, new land to the extent of 50 per cent of land under cultivation at present will be cultivated; railway mileage will be increased by 50 per cent, roads enlarged 150 per cent, extensive public work, particularly irrigation, construction of houses to provide decent living conditions to the rural population and the working and middle classes in cities and towns; building of schools and hospitals".[9]

According to Roy, "Without political planning, economic planning is found to be an idle speculation".[10] A really democratic government should be established in India where people will be in effective control of political power. Then only planned economy would be possible. People's plan was followed by the Draft Constitution of Free India. The Draft visualises a democratic State, the supreme power rests with the people.

Roy came to realise that *party system* and *power politics* were not the solution for relieving the people from their problems, in his last phase of life. In order to bring about a social revolution, he propounded the philosophy of New Humanism. In it, the individual would be independent unit of society. To quote S.R. Das, "Man is freedom loving, romantic and creative animal. He would submit to no domination, dictation or bondage. So, it would be the task of the co-operative commonwealth to give every individual opportunities for direct participation in the governance of the State through the Panchayats".[11]

Roy believed that *New Humanism* could be a substitute to capitalism, based on competitive economy, on one side; and to communism, based on collective economy on the other. He believed in direct democracy in the form of a network of small cooperative commonwealths. His New Humanism is based on decentralisation and cooperation. In it, man would enjoy his freedom as well as his security. To him, the cooperative economy should be guided by two considerations: (1) the basic purpose of national economy is to provide food, shelter and clothing for the people, and (2) one must cut the coat according to the cloth available. The people would conduct and coordinate the economic activities of the society through consumers and producers cooperatives. The village would be a suitable unit. He said, "The working population of the village can, thus, form itself into a cooperative community for all the three purposes of estate management, farming operations and the running of the village industries".[12]

Commodities will have to be exchanged and local multipurpose cooperative societies will be integrated into one larger economic system. *Large scale industries* would be developed with the help of the surplus pooled by the local cooperatives. Roy observed, "Built on the basis of a cooperative agriculture and locally developed industries, the super-structure of the large scale production of certain specified articles or exploitation of natural resources, such as mining, will also be cooperative. They will be owned by cooperative societies—the new source of capital formation".[13] The private owned industries would also have the option to join the cooperative system or to remain independent and compete with cooperative economy.

Roy gave the first importance to agriculture rather than to industrialisation in India in his planning. To him, the recognition and development of agriculture as the foundation of a healthy rational modern economy stands a greater change than any other method to succeed in removing the poverty of the Indian people. He favoured the cooperative method of farming. According to him, capitalism, socialism, communism and welfare State etc., were unable to give freedom, democracy and security to the individual. The only alternative was New Humanism (cooperative socialism).

REFERENCES

1. M.N. Roy, *India in Transition*, Edition de la Librarie J.B. Target, Geneva, 1922, p. 56.
2. A.K. Hindi, *M.N. Roy: The Man Who Looked Ahead*, Vol. I, The Modern Publishing House, Ahmedabad, 1938, p, 132.
3. M.N. Roy, *Letters by M.N. Roy to the Congress Socialist Party*, The Renaissance Publishing Company, Bombay, 1937, p. 6.
4. M.N. Roy and Evelyn Roy, *One Year of Non-cooperation: From Ahmedabad to Gaya*, Communist Party of India, Calcutta, 1923, pp. 105-11.
5. A.K. Hindi, *M.N. Roy: The Man Who Looked Ahead*, *op. cit.*, pp. 200-01.
6. L.P. Sinha—Abstract, cited in R.K. Awasthi, *Scientific Humanism,*

Socio-Political Ideas of M.N. Roy (A critique), College Book Depot, Jaipur, p. 13.

7. M.N. Roy, *Scientific Politics,* The Indian Renaissance Association Limited, Dehradun, 1942, p. 116.
8. *Ibid.*, p. 147.
9. M.N. Roy, *Peoples' Plan for Economic Development of India*, Indian Federation of Labour, Delhi, 1944, pp. 6-7.
10. M.N. Roy, *Planning A New India*, Renaissance Publishers, Calcutta, p. 49.
11. K.C. Jena, *Contributions of M.N. Roy to Political Philosophy*, S. Chand and Company, 1968, p. 114.
12. *The Radical Humanist*, 11-7-1954, p. 328.
13. M.N. Roy, *New Humanism: A Manifesto*, Renaissance Publishers, Calcutta, 1953, p. 53.

11

ROY ON DEMOCRACY

M.N. Roy criticises Parliamentary democracy. He thinks that *Parliamentary democracy* is no democracy at all. It is not the government of the people, by the people but on behalf of the people. The sovereign individuals in practice remain passive spectators. After elections, individuals have no control over their representatives. Individuals are ruled by a group of partymen. *Democracy* is converted into dictatorship of Cabinet. He also criticises election system in Parliamentary democracy. To him, representatives are not elected intelligently. Man is lost in the crowd and elections take place playing upon the crowd mentality. Persons, who are elected, are those who know how to play on mass mentality. He agrees that democracy is converted into *demagogy*.

Roy was of the opinion that the greatest fault of Parliamentary democracy is its inherent tendency toward centralisation of power. He was the champion of maximum *decentralisation*. To him, centralisation of power leads to a dehumanisation process. Wherein all the powers are centralised in the executive and important decisions are taken by the executive, bureaucracy and committees of the experts. Even the representatives of the people have no say in it, and are reduced to a mere rubber stamp.

Roy rejects the idea that parties are co-present with *politics*. Political parties imply the denial of *sovereignty* of the individual and democracy. He feels that representative government is in effect only a minority government. To him, it represents only the party, which controls it and membership, even of the largest party, is only a small fraction of the people. Thus, democracy is a government by a party and not by the people.

As an alternative to Parliamentary democracy, Roy presents his scheme of government based on the principles of *decentralisation*, individual freedom and popular participation. He suggests a pyramidal structure of Indian polity reared on the basis of an organised democracy composed of a countrywide network of Peoples' Committees. To him, the government will become coterminous with society.

Roy gives full sovereign rights to the individuals including the right to recall their representatives. He gives emphasis on economic decentralisation. He agrees that the new democracy cannot be built in a day or two. There will be transition period during which conditions will be created to introduce new democracy. He agrees that education of the individual is of seminal importance for the success of true *democracy*. To him, individual must be oriented, made conscious and moral by education. He holds the view that during the period of election campaign, masses may be educated, and insist that education should be imparted by non-governmental agencies.

Roy believed that India came under foreign rule because it was culturally backward and not that its cultural backwardness resulted from foreign rule. He regarded that the very spiritual heritage of India which was upheld and applauded by Indian nationalists was the cause of India's cultural decay.

In Roy's conception of *organised democracy* the State will be coincident with the entire society, and consequently, it will be under a standing democratic control. He does not feel it necessary to abolish it.

Roy had criticised the functioning of *Parliamentary democracy* in the modern world. Political parties are inevitable in his scheme of democracy and its mechanism of election. He based his new organised polity on the principle of political decentralisation.

Roy accepted the popular definition of *democracy* as a government of the people, by the people and for the people. He advocated democracy because, of its belief in individual freedom and sovereignty of the people. He said, "All talk of democracy; yet no where do we find government of the people, by the people. There is a big discrepancy between the theoretical ideas and ideals evolved in the nineteenth century and the actual picture of today".[1] Regarding Parliamentary democracy, he was of the opinion that it is not a democracy at all. He said, "If democracy means government of the people and by the people, the democratic experiment has been a dismal failure. Modern democratic governments are neither governments of the people nor by the people; they are governments for the people, which means the people are not ruled by themselves and therefore, Parliamentary governments are not democratic governments".[2]

Roy blamed the Rousseau's theory of general will, which sought to bridge the gulf between theory and practice of *Parliamentary democracy*. It led to dictatorship. He said, "There are some millions of people with will of their own. But there is one general will of the nation, which is more important than the wills of all the people, who compose the nation".[3]

The sovereign individual in practice remains a passive spectator in Parliamentary democracy. Roy remarked, "In Parliamentary democracy, power nominally belongs to the entire people. But in practice the individual is divested of all power; the individual is helpless in parliamentary democracy".[4] Again he said, "Parliamentary democracy formally recognised the sovereignty of the individual, but in practice deprived all but a privileged few of effective use of that sovereignty. The sovereign individual become a legal fiction. For all practical purposes, most individuals were deprived of all power and even of their dignity".[5]

To Roy, the practice of *delegation of power* is a negation of democracy. It means surrender of sovereignty. To him, parliamentary democracy is nothing more than the government for the people in which the people are always ignored and their role is only to cast a vote in favour of a particular candidate after four or five years.

The only guarantee for democracy is that power must always remain in the hands of people. Roy said, "As soon as, on one pretext or another, power is taken away from the people by delegation, even for the shortest period of time, democracy is killed".[6] To him, delegation of power to the representatives by the voters is the curse of parliamentary democracy. He said, "For parliamentary democracy implies delegation of sovereign power which originally belongs to the individual. The individual robbed off his sovereignty, is reduced to the position of a mere cog in the wheel, once his sovereign power is delegated, first to a body of legislators, and thereafter to the executive which is further removed from the body of representatives".[7]

According to Roy, *centralisation* of power leads to dehumanisation of the individuals. He said, "One weakness of parliamentary democracy is that it leads to great concentration of power in the hands of executive viz., Cabinet. Under modern conditions control of *Parliament* over the cabinet has become extremely tenuous, the cabinet form of government does by no means foster genuine democratic leadership. The government by an all powerful committee may easily degenerate into a short personal dictatorship, if the Prime Minister who presides over this committee happens to be a towering personality head and shoulder above his colleagues".[8]

Political parties are said to be necessary for its success in Parliamentary democracy. According to Roy, political parties have very recent origin. They are not co-present with politics. He said, "These who identify democracy with the party system overlook the fact that political parties are relatively recent institutions. Political parties as we know them today are a development only of the nineteenth century, when the doctrine of representative government replaced the earlier idea of democracy. Parliamentarism, based on the theory of the delegation of power to elected representatives, made of democracy a mere formality".[9]

According to Roy, Political parties try to capture power by any means. He said, "A party is organised with the object of capturing power. It is done with the ostensibly possible argument that some people know just how society should be organised, therefore, the voters must vote for them so that they come to power and impose the blessings they have in mind from above on the people, who could otherwise never even think of those blessings, much less achieve them on their own".[10] Further he said, "Party politics implies the denial of democracy; it implies that people cannot do anything by themselves; it is a denial of the potential intelligence and creativity of all men, of the sovereignty of the people".[11]

According to Roy, democracy has degenerated into demogogy. He observed, "Under the democratic system a party can come to power only with the consent of the people. It is quite evident and that was also the experience in practice that any part which could make the most glittering promises had the greatest chance of obtaining the consent of the people. The result was that democracy degenerated into demogogy".[12] He believed that political parties leads to concentration of power and hence carries in it the germs of the destruction of democracy.

The Party system leads to complete erosion of the status of individual from the political scene. Roy remarked, "The individual man and his judgement, his discretion and will are nowhere in the picture. Appeals are not made to individual voters and their power of reasoning, but to the sentiment of masses. The purpose of election propaganda is to create a state of mass hysteria, to create either hatred for one or bias in favour of some other party. Consequently, when the time comes for the sovereign people to make the crucial decision of selecting persons, who can be entrusted with their fate for a period of four or five years, the electorate is in a state where no discriminating judgement is at all possible, whipped up into a state of frenzy and driven like cattle to the polling stations to cast their votes. With music, brassbands, flags and shouting, the judgment of the people is dulled and benumbed; they are placed under some spell and in that condition they are asked to decide their fate".[13]

The *individual* is forgotten in party system and the attention is shifted to an unbecoming process of power game. Roy said, "Modern Parliamentary democracy is degenerated into a scramble for power among party machineries. Different parties approach the people with the claim to represent them more faithfully than others, to be better defenders of popular interests and aspirations, and, therefore, ask for the vote of the people. Under the best of circumstances, these parties alternate in power and divide the government between themselves. Government of the people and by the people is completely forgotten and has been replaced by government for the people; in other words, it is not a really democratic form of government".[14]

According to Roy, with the rise of the political parties in modern States, the idea of popular *sovereignty* has disappeared. He said, "With the rise of the party system, the idea of popular sovereignty became a constitutional fiction. The party system resulted from the difficulty of practising direct democracy in large modern States with numerous populations. And with the rise of party system, politics became a scramble for power".[15] Party system gives importance to those individuals who can be instrumental in capturing power. Roy remarked, "Under such circumstances, the sovereignty of the individual becomes meaningless; democracy demands that the sovereign individual must merge himself in a party, be a subservient part of an impersonal party machine. In an atmosphere of political backwardness and general ignorance, this system can be abused; people of questionable character can occupy positions of public trust by virtue of belonging to a political party".[16]

Roy was of the opinion that parliamentary democracy

could not solve the problem of poverty. He said, "An economy that starves the fixed income group and fills the coffers of the unscrupulous few and starves millions in depression by throwing them on the street, cannot command the respect of humanity for long. All the beautiful names like free enterprise or free economy given to it cannot obliterate the moral revolution roused by facts like the destruction of food and other commodities in surplus areas, while the people go hungry elsewhere".[17]

Roy criticised the free economy, which is exercised under the parliamentary democracy, but he does not fully agree with the socialist criticism of parliamentary democracy is nothing but a fraud, *liberty* has no meaning, and it is a democracy of the rich few who exploit the poor. To him, equality is an ethical proposition rather than economic. Parliamentary democracy is not only full of inadequacies but it is dangerous also, because it leads to *totalitarianism*.

Roy suggested the formation of Radical Democracy. It is based on *decentralisation* and elimination of political parties. To quote R.K. Awasthi, "It provides a scheme of government without political parties. Decentralisation and diffusion of power would be its method of operation. Helping to secure and all-round development of individual personality guaranteeing the dignity of the individual and *freedom* in its widest connotation would be its end".[18] He opines that under his conception of radical democracy, the principle of government of the people and by the people will be practicable in the modern world. Roy said, "Even in large political units and highly complex social organisations of the modern world direct democracy will be possible in the form of a network of small cooperative commonwealths, which will replace the helpless atomised voter of formal parliamentary democracy".[19]

There is no place for political parties in Roy's scheme of radical democracy. He erected the structure of *Partyless democracy* through the mechanism of people's committees. He has accorded the supreme status to the individual in the society. He said, "No scheme of decentralisation is likely to work unless there is a philosophical revolution and the individual has known that he is the architect of his own destiny".[20] To him, radical democracy is a government composed of spiritually free individuals accountable, in the first place, to their respective conscience. The leaders will function as guides, friends and philosophers of the people.

According to Roy, the foundation of the State is organised through the *people's committees*. But all authority is to emanate from the people. The basic feature of radical democracy is that the people must have ways and means to exercise sovereign power effectively. For this, he recommended a vigorous system of local government.

The primary function of the local people's committees will be to make individual citizens fully conscious of intelligently and consciously. People's committees are to exercise real power and representatives in the Assembly and Parliament will be merely their spokesman. Roy said, "And at the election time, when all parties come and offer their candidates, the People's committees may decide to vote for none of those Party candidates and the people will vote for him. The person who will be thus elected and go to the Parliament will not be responsible to any existing political party machinery. He will be and remain responsible to his local democracy, of which he himself is a part; he will be directly responsible to the people who sent him to the parliament; he will not have to act on the behests and discipline of any extraneous authority and he will have to report to and inform his fellow citizens in his constituency about all his actions and the problems of the wider community, and take his mandate from them alone in all matters and act accordingly to his best ability and conscience".[21]

The people will have the right to alter and modify the political organisation of the society. They will also have right to revolt against tyranny and opression. Roy said, "People's

Committees will create conditions that will stimulate amongst the people the urge for freedom, the desire to rely on themselves, and to be makers of their own destiny, the spirit of free thinking, and they will never submit to any external authority by exchanging their *freedom* for the security of slaves. A new renaissance based on *rationalism, individualism* and *cosmopolitan humanism* is essential for democracy to be realised and capable of defending itself".[22]

The change from party politics to politics without parties would be brought about gradually by raising the intellectual level of the people. Roy remarked, "It does without saying that this changeover cannot take place from today to tomorrow; nor will an entire country discard the old practice and adopt the new one all at once. It will be a process, and the process itself will be uneven. This changeover from party politics to democratic politics will be brought about gradually by raising the intellectual level of the people, by quickening their sense of self-respect and self-reliance. Therefore, democracy is not possible without education".[23] He preferred Parliamentary democracy to a dictatorship in the transitional period. To him, in the transitional phase, the spiritually free men would guide and lead the functioning of the governmental machinery. He said, "Values operate through individuals, therefore, a government composed of spiritually free individuals, accountable, in the first place, to their respective conscience, is the only possible guarantee for securing the greatest good of the greatest number. *Democracy* must have that philosophical reorientation, if it is to survive the present crisis and resist the powerful onslaught of dictatorship".[24]

The radical democracy presupposes the economic reorganisation of society. The economic reorganisation of society should be as to eliminate the possibility of exploitation of man. Progressive satisfaction of material necessities is the precondition for the individual members of society unfolding their intellectual and other finer human attributes, said Roy. The production would be for use and the distribution according to human needs.

Roy pointed out that *education* was a precondition for the success of democracy. He observed, "The original sin of the discredit democratic practice was to forget the wisdom of Plato who said that education was the condition for democracy".[25] He stood for a philosophical revolution, without which no social change in the direction of greater freedom is possible. He suggested that even parliamentary democracy should be introduced only when people are prepared for it.

According to Roy, the ability and training of individual to develop and realise his own potentiality, rationality and responsibility is known as education. He said, "Education for democracy does not consist in teaching just reading and writing, but in making people conscious of their humanness, in making them conscious of their right to exist as human beings, in decency and dignity. Education means to help them to think, to apply their reason".[26] He was against the compulsory government sponsored *education*. He said, "The purpose of government education is to create mental confirmism. You have to sing patriotic songs, salute national flags and read patriotic history as compiled and edited by governments, so that all people be merged into a homogeneous collectivity and forget that they are individuals endowed with certain sovereign faculties and entitled to be free".[27] Education must create faith in a man in himself.

REFERENCES

1. M.N. Roy, *Politics, Power and Parties,* Renaissance Publishers, Calcutta, 1960, p. 5.
2. M.N. Roy, *The Problem of Freedom*, Renaissance Publishers, Calcutta, 1945, p. 134.
3. *The Radical Humanist*, 19-8-1956, p. 391.
4. M.N. Roy, *Beyond Communism*, Renaissance Publishers, Calcutta, 1968, p. 119.
5. M.N. Roy, *Politics, Power and Parties, op. cit.*, p. 19.

6. M.N. Roy, *Politics, Power and Parties*, p. 84.
7. *The Radical Humanist*, March 1956, p. 99.
8. *The Radical Humanist*, 2-9-1956, p. 411.
9. M.N. Roy, *Politics, Power and Parties*, *op. cit.*, p. 67.
10. *Ibid.*, p. 63.
11. *Ibid.*, p. 63.
12. Kiran Saxena, *Modern Indian Political Thought: Gandhism and Roy's New Humanism*, Chetna Publishers, New Delhi, 1978, p. 138.
13. M.N. Roy, *Politics, Power and Parties*, *op. cit.*, p. 52.
14. *Ibid.*, p. 53.
15. *The Radical Humanist*, 4-6-1950, p. 259.
16. *Ibid.*, p. 68.
17. *Ibid.*, 1-11-1953, p. 528.
18. R.K. Awasthi, *Scientific Humanism, Socio-Political Ideas of M.N. Roy*, College Book Depot, Jaipur, p. 208.
19. B.S. Sharma, *The Political Philosophy of M.N. Roy*, National Publishing House, Delhi, 1965, p. 83.
20. R.K. Awasthi, *Scientific Humanism*, *op. cit.*, p. 210.
21. M.N. Roy, *Politics, Power and Parties*, *op. cit.*, p. 60.
22. M.N. Roy, *New Humanism*, *op. cit.*, p. 45.
23. M.N. Roy, *Politics, Power and Parties*, *op. cit.*, p. 95.
24. M.N. Roy, *New Humanism*, *op. cit.*, p. 44.
25. M.N. Roy, *Politics, Power and Parties*, *op. cit.*, p. 117.
26. *Ibid.*, p. 173.
27. *Ibid.*, p. 59.

12

ROY ON PEACE

M.N. Roy was an advocate of world peace. He criticised *communism, imperialism, fascism* and other expansionist systems. He laid stress on principles of self-determination, non-involvement and non-interference. He condemned war as a means to settle disputes. He reacted promptly to the issues involving *violence* and suppression. He condemned the big powers and advised the Indian Government to remain aloof. He criticised the competitive race for armament.

Roy criticised nationalism. To him, the spirit of nationalism was the main cause behind the wars. To avoid the fear of wars, he proposed to abolish the national boundary lines and to create a *cosmopolitan* commonwealth of freemen and women. He justified the Second World War. It was an international people's war. He pleaded for assistance to Britain in the war. He was the only Indian thinker who supported the war efforts of Britain.

Roy was an advocate of world unity for cultural salvation of mankind at large. He believed that the struggle for national freedom has an international dimension. He criticised the idea of *Nationalism* and *Fascism*. His New Humanism offered a remedy to the problems of international relations. He criticised nationalism for breeding racial hatred. He said, "It is reactionary and devoid of any social purpose. Its motivative force is racial animosity, which is glorified or rationalised on the plea of conflict and culture. And the so-called cultural nationalism, in its turn, aggravates the racial bias of nationalist politics. The fiction of social and cultural unity is dramatised to distract people's attention from the facts of social inequality".[1] The idea of Nationalism has divided the world into small national boundaries. The Nationalism was like the philosophy of frog in the well.

Roy was of the opinion that national freedom would not mean *freedom* of the entire community. He appealed to the Indian nationalists to participate in a spirit of cosmopolitanism and cooperation with other peoples. He criticised the theory of *Nationalism* propounded by Gandhi. He said, "The people who are proudly teaching the cult of the Mahatma should not forget that their own nationalism is taking them further and further away, day by day, from this very teachings, because their nationalism demands a powerful army, and all the latest equipments of warfare and military defence, and the demand is being increasingly taken for granted by all patriots and nationalists in the country".[2]

Roy believed in the cooperative fellowships of man. His *New Humanism* is pledged to the ideal of a commonwealth and fraternity of freedom. He said, "New Humanism is cosmopolitan. A cosmopolitan commonwealth of spiritually freemen would not be limited by the boundaries of national States—capitalist, fascist, socialist, communist, or any other kind, which will gradually disappear under the impact of the twentieth century renaissance of man".[3] He supported the ideal of internationalism. Under it, the backward and underdeveloped countries would not be exploited further by the rich countries. He criticised socialism and communism.

Roy made a distinction between *cosmopolitanism* and *internationalism*. He pleaded for cosmopolitan humanism. He said, "No effort, however, bombastic and expensive, on the governmental level can take the world out of the present impasse. The hope lies in human endeavour; the cultural sanction of national States must be progressively withheld by a growing number of individual men and women in each country outgrowing the tribal mentality and cultivating the spirit of cosmopolitan Humanism. That is the only hope".[4]

According to Roy, *fascism* constitutes a big hurdle in the way of world peace and unity. To him, fascism was the highest form of nationalism. He said, "Nationalism necessarily culminates in *fascism* which carries the metaphysical conception of State to its absurd climax. Fascism lays bare the totalitarian essence of the concept of nation, as something distinct from the people—a collectivity which exists and thrives at the cost of the individuals composing it".[5] To him, reactionary nationalism is an integral part of international fascism. He regarded fascism as the logical outcome of post-Hegalian idealism. Fascism culminates into a spiritual philosophy of expediency. The most important characteristic feature of Fascism was the cult of super man, and this was present in the Indian leadership tradition. He regarded Nehru as the standard bearer of Congress nationalism.

Roy considered the Second World War as a war between *democracy* and *totalitarianism*. He believed that the war would put an end to the cult of fascism. The destruction of fascism was necessary for freedom. To him, the end of fascism might coincide with the end of imperialism in India. The Second World War was not an imperialist war but an international civil war. He replaced Lenin's conception of imperialist war by his theory of international civil war. In the wake of nuclear weapons, he felt that if the third world war happened, it would mean the end of human civilisation. He said, "One does not require a very high degree of imaginativeness to realise that another world war will have the most disastrous consequences, most probably amounting to a complete breakdown of modern civilisation. The greatest possible efforts must be made to head off that threatening catastrophe".[6]

Roy condemned the Russian Communism and considered American democracy as a lesser evil. He never favoured the use of military forces as a means to check the expansion of *Communism*. He criticised the American foreign policy, which stressed on military potential to check the Communism. He believed that if every country were allowed to choose their form of government without the interference from outside, the world peace would remain undisturbed. He criticised the power blocs.

Roy was a strong advocate of international peace and maintained that peace at any price is the sanest policy for all but the lunatic. The problem of *democracy* versus *communism* could only be solved by peaceful means. As an alternative to groupism and power bloc rivalries, he suggested the practice of New Humanism. According to him, a world composed of nation States can never be peaceful. He envisaged the idea of a cosmopolitan cooperative commonwealth of creative men. He attached great importance to the objective of world peace and brotherhood. He condemned the use of brute force as a means of settling the international disputes.

REFERENCES

1. M.N. Roy, *The Problem of Freedom*, Renaissance Publishers, Calcutta, 1945, p. 113.
2. *The Radical Humanist*, Vol. XXIV, No. 6, 7-2-1962, p. 65.
3. M.N. Roy, *Reason, Romanticism and Revolution*, Renaissance Publishers, Calcutta, 1955, p. 310.
4. *The Radical Humanist*, Vol. XIII, 1-5-1949, p. 204.
5. M.N. Roy, *The Problem of Freedom*, *op. cit.*, pp. 97-98.
6. M.N. Roy, *Reason, Romanticism and Revolution*, *op. cit.*, p. 275.

13

READINGS FROM ROY

If man was ideal, there would be nothing for us to do. In quest of freedom, in search of knowledge, he blundered into all sorts of wrong channels and conceived false ideas; therefore, his entire mental make-up is much burdened with heaps of ballast. When we talk about education and enlightenment, of making man moral, we undertake the task of removing the heaps of ballast which have buried the innate *rationality* of man. In proportion as we succeed in removing that ballast, we shall succeed in showing up the rationality in man. We only say that man is essentially rational; that is an assumption as well as an empirical deduction. As assumption it is corroborated by the scientific knowledge that man is part of a law-governed universe.

—*Independent India*,
4-1-1948

We subjected the materialist philosophy, as formulated on the basis of the scientific knowledge of eighteenth century and nineteenth centuries, to a searching analysis in the light of the latest discoveries of science. The analysis revealed fallacies and deficiencies which, however, did not invalidate the basic principles of *materialism*. It is not a closed system of thought—a bunch of dogmas. It is a logical coordination and integration of empirical knowledge into an all-embracing explanation of existence. Therefore, it requires continuous readjustment, amplification, enrichment and precision.

—*Independent India*,
20-6-1948

We must speak the *language* of the people; look at the problems from their point of view, from the experience of daily life. Fortunately they are not corrupted by the perversions of modern scientific knowledge as preached by some semi-educated middle class. Scientific knowledge can be brought to them in a simple language. The old theories of the nineteenth century may be naive for the highbrow who cannot see the relation between science and life. Steam still has power; electricity can be harnessed for the benefit of man; medicine cures; biology explains a whole lot of things of daily experience; *Darwinism* is still to go to the masses, particularly in our country; psychology throws light on the mysteries of mental life. The people, particularly in our country, require this kind of knowledge; it will give them a sense of power, their moral stamina will be reinforced in proportion as knowledge liberates them from the traditional bondage of ignorance fostered on the authority of religion.

Nor is it necessary for the people to grasp intricate problems of *sociology*; the breakdown of the economic system is a matter of experience. It is not necessary for them to understand economic theories. They experience want when there is no reason for it. Once they are made conscious of their experience, they will feel the need for a reconstruction. Political problems can be similarly accessible to them in experience. Finally we shall show them how they can take things in their own hands. But all these easy steps presuppose man's faith in himself. They will gain faith also in the experience of doing things.

—*Independent India*,
12-9-1948

Popular political parties operate with slogans: agitate, educate and organise. But until now none has educated or organised. Experience shows that agitation precludes education; and mobilisation is not to organise. The replacement of atomised democracy by organised democracy presupposes emphasis on education. Only an educated democracy can be an organised democracy. Therefore, we hold that democracy is not possible without education; that education is the foundation of democracy. Political *education* of the people is not very helpful for the old political parties, right or left. The practice of opposition parties, either parliamentary or insurrectionary, does not lead to the establishment of democratic government. It is clear that our activities cannot be cast in the pattern of activities of other parties which are following that objective. We need not think that all others are scoundrels and we angels. Placed in similar situations, we ourselves may also turn out to be scoundrels. One is bound by the laws of the world in which one lives, and if we breathe in the atmosphere of the world of power-politics, we shall be bound by its laws.

—*Independent India*,
19-12-1948

Though presented here as a political philosophy, *New Humanism* is meant to be a complete system. Based on the ever expanding totality of scientific knowledge, it cannot be a closed system. It will not be a logical integration of the knowledge about the various aspects of existence, showing how it is in the nature of man to be rational and moral, and, therefore, capable of building a free, harmonious and just social order.

—*New Humanism*,
p. viii

Radicalism thinks in terms neither of nation nor of class; its concern is man; it conceives freedom as freedom of the individual. Therefore, it can also be called New Humanism, new because it is Humanism enriched, reinforced and elaborated by scientific knowledge and social experience gained during the centuries of modern civilisation..

—*New Humanism*,
p. 34

Values operate through individuals. Therefore, a government composed of spiritually free individuals, accountable in the first place to their respective conscience, is the only possible guarantee for securing the greatest good to the greatest number. *Democracy* must have that philosophical orientation, if it is to survive the present crisis and resist the powerful onslaught of dictatorship.

What is suggested is not a rule of the intellectual elite, but such an organisation of society as will give unlimited scope for the unfolding of the creative genius of man by placing the executive power of the State under the control of free individuals—free from the influence of vested interests and also from vagaries of the collective ego, so very susceptive to *demogogic* appeals.

—*New Humanism*,
p. 42

No party which joins in the struggle (for power) can win and yet remain democratic either in its internal organisation or in its attitude to, and influence on, the people. Consequently once the power is captured by any party, it is never diffused. Pursuit of power, even when undertaken as a means to its diffusion, defeats the purpose.

—*New Humanism*,
p. 64

Throughout the course of history, the spiritual revolts have always proceeded great social changes. Mental freedom has necessarily been the precondition for any attempt to attain political and economic freedom. Faced with economic insufficiency, political oppression and social instability, the people can nevertheless develop the will as well as the ability to change that situation. *Scientific Humanism* precludes the view that the will to freedom and the ability to attain it are accessible only to a minority, which is thus qualified for leadership.

—*New Humanism*,
p. 66

Anthropology also helps us in the inquiry into human nature. It proves that human society did not originate in an ad-hoc control. Primitive man had to struggle against his environment. He could do so more successfully in cooperation with others. The instinct of self-preservation and struggle for existence led to the foundation of civil society. Instinct is primitive reason. Man, therefore, is essentially a rational being.

Modern knowledge of biology also allows this deduction. Rudiments of reason, the ability to connet experiences, can be traced in lower animals. Rationality, therefore, is a biological function which can very highly develop in the highest biological form. *Rationality* can subordinate man's selfishness to enlightened self-interest, which is a social virtue.

—*New Humanism*,
p. 90

Let us not be utopians. Ideas are never completely attained. We can only achieve a greater or lesser approximation towards an ideal. The end of the basic human urge is to approximate to the greatest possible extent the ideal of freedom. If *freedom* is defined as the progressive elimination of all restrictions on the unfoldment of the potentialities latent in man, it ceases to be an abstraction, and can be intimately and concretely related with the daily affairs of human life.

—*Politics, Power and Parties*, p. 24

Not only the politicians, but even the people themselves have come to doubt that they can wield power and exercise their *sovereignty*. They have forgotten that all men are born with the same potentialities, the highest being that of their reasoning faculty. The way out, which party politicians would not take, because that would mean the end of their days, is an appeal to reason. That appeal has the sanction of modern *science* behind it. Human nature is rational. It is true that the rational nature of man has been buried fathoms deep. But being the essence of human nature, it can be recovered. Unreason has gone so far that the appeal to reason is bound to find response, and a rational political practice will bear fruit sooner than one might imagine. But the measure of success will not be power; it will be gradual disappearance of the evils which are at the root of the present situation. It will express itself in an intelligent public opinion which cannot be swayed by emotional and demagogic appeals.

—*Politics, Power and Parties*, p. 77

The problem of democracy can, therefore, no longer be solved by political parties. It is a deeper and more comprehensive problem than one of institutional adjustments. It can be solved only by a comprehensive social movement developed on the basis of the ultimate identity of political, economic and moral problems, and inspired by a philosophy capable of suggesting solutions of them all. *New Humanism* of which *Radical Democracy* is the political expression, is such a philosophy. Guided by this philosophy Radical Democrats will now endeavour to develop a Radical Humanist Movement, and in consequence discard a form of organisation which had become irrelevant to their task.

—*Politics, Power and Parties*, p. 94

Rising out of the background of the physical universe, man incorporates the best of creation. If there is any creative power, that is in him. It is held by many that man is bad, immoral unthinking and, therefore, there is no hope for the world. But the present knowledge about man allows the proposition that man is essentially rational. Every human behaviour, in the last analysis, is rational, however, irrational it may appear. Morality results from man's intelligent response to his surroundings. Therefore, it can be deduced from his innate rationality. Since *rationality* is inherent in human nature, it is only necessary to remind him of his biological heritage, and he will regain faith in himself and undo the harm done to him. Having realised the mistakes of the past, and trying to rectify them, modern mankind will find a way out of the crisis of our time, and begin marching forward to much greater achievements than those of the past.

—*Reason, Romanticism and Revolution*, p. 272

According to the view which traces human development on the highest level to the subsoil of human existence, human nature is essentially rational. The original creation of society was a rational act. Perhaps, a number of our predecessors, as yet hardly differentiated from their annual ancestry, struggling for existence against wild beasts, saw that all of them did the same thing and realised that, if they acted together, they could combat the common enemies with greater chance of success. That rational judgement led to the foundation of civil society.

This human instinct can be traced further down in the process of biological evolution. What is called instinct is only a primitive form of *rationalism*. This knowledge of the mechanism of biological evolution leads to the conclusion that human nature is essentially *rational*. But in course of time, various other views of life developed, which made man forget that they are rational. To believe in supernatural powers appeared to be the fundamental trait of human nature. Consistent with that belief, the human being itself is not capable of judging what is good and what is bad, a harmonious relation between the individual and society is not possible. There may be harmony, but it will be coercive. If we have a community fully sharing certain beliefs, then we may have a harmonious society, but it may not be a free society. Because, if a member of that community suddenly begins to doubt that any particular belief which he had been taught may perhaps not be true and wants to investigate if that belief is really correct, he immediately becomes an element of discord—the harmony is disturbed. To maintain harmony, his freedom must be curtailed or he will be expelled from the society. So, either society ceases to be harmonious or it decomposes.

—*Radical Humanist,*
31-10-1954

We do not say anything new when we demand that man must be the measure of everything. One of the founders of philosophy, Protagoras, said that already more than 2500 years ago. Yet mankind seems to have forgotten its soul. The same liberalising principle was repeated by Karl Marx, who is today honoured as the prophet of proletarian *dictatorship*, the advocates of which fanatically demand sacrifice of the individual at the altar of an imaginary collective ego. Karl Marx said: "Man is the root of mankind". That was even more explicit than what Protagoras had demanded as the criterion of all values. Karl Marx could improve upon the ancient sage, because he had greater scientific knowledge at his disposal. What does the principle mean? First comes man, then mankind; the individual is antecedent to society, which is the means for the unfolding of his potentialities in continuation of the process of pre-human biological evolution. The end should not be sacrificed to the means; the position of the individual is the measure of social progress. That is the philosophical essence of Marxism, the collectivist interpretation of which has become a form of totalitarianism.

—*Beyond Communism,*
p. 132

BIBLIOGRAPHY

Agrawal, A.N., *Socialism Without Prejudice*, Kitabistan, Allahabad, 1947.

Ahmed, I., *Trends in Socialistic Thought Movement*, The Indian Press, Allahabad, 1937.

Awasthi, R.K., *Scientific Humanism: Socio-Political Ideas of M.N. Roy: A Critique*, College Book Depot, Jaipur.

Bali. D.R., *Modern Indian Thought From Ram Mohan Roy to M.N.* Roy, Sterling Publishers Private Limited, New Delhi, 1980.

Bhattacharjee, G.P., *Evolution of Political Philosophy of M.N. Roy*, The Minerva Associates, Calcutta, 1971.

Bhattacharjee, G.P., *M.N. Roy and Radical Humanism*, J.B.H. Wadia Publications, Bombay, 1961.

Blackham, H.J., *M.N. Roy: Philosopher Revolutionary*, Renaissance Publishers, Calcutta, 1956.

Cole, G.D.H., *The Simple Case for Socialism*, Victor Gollanez Limited, London, 1935.

Das, R.S., *M.N. Roy—The Humanist Philosopher*, R.S. Das, Calcutta, 1959.

Datta, A., *The Way to Co-operative Socialism*, The Radical Humanist Publication, Calcutta.

Dhar, N., *The Political Thought of M.N. Roy*, Eureka Publishers, Calcutta, 1966.

Ghosh, S., *Socialism and Communism in India*, Allied Publishers, Bombay, 1971.

Ghosh, S., *Socialism, Democracy and Nationalism in India*, Allied Publishers, Bombay, 1973.

Grover, D.C., *M.N. Roy: Revolution and Reason in Indian*

Politics, The Minerva Associates, Calcutta, 1973.

Gupta, B.N., *M.N. Roy: Quest for Freedom,* Firma, K.L. Mukhopadhyaya, Calcutta.

Gupta, S.D., *Total Revolution—A Symposium*, Naya Prakash, Calcutta, 1978.

Gupta, R.C., *Socialism, Democracy and India*, Ram Prasad & Sons, Agra, 1965.

Hindi, A.K., *M.N. Roy: The Man Who Looked Ahead*, The Modern Publishing House, Ahmedabad, 1938.

Jena, K.C., *Contributions of M.N. Roy to Political Philosophy*, S. Chand and Company, Delhi, 1968.

Karnik, V.B., *M.N. Roy: Political Biography*, Nava Jagriti Samaj, Bombay, 1978.

Mahajan, V.D., *Recent Political Thought*, S. Chand & Company, New Delhi, 1956.

Maron, S., *Power and Purpose*, Renaissance Publishers, Calcutta, 1963.

Masani, M.R., *Socialism Reconsidered*, Padma Publications, Bombay, 1944.

Nigam, R.L., *Radical Humanism of M.N. Roy*, Indus Publishing Company, New Delhi, 1988.

Ojha, V.N., *Roy and his Philosophical Ideas*, Shankhand Prakashan, Muzaffarpur, 1969.

Prasad, R.A., *Socialist Thought in Modern India*, Meenakshi Prakashan, Meerut, 1974.

Ray, S., *Radicalism*, Renaissance Publishers, Calcutta, 1946.

Ray, S., *M.N. Roy: Philosopher Revolutionary*, Renaissance Publishers, Calcutta, 1959.

Roy, M.N., *The Aftermath of Non-Cooperation*, The Communist Party of Great Britain, London, 1926.

Roy, M.N., *The Future of Indian Politics*, R. Bishop, London, 1926.

Roy, M.N., *Our Task in India*, B.C.R.P.I.W.C., Calcutta, 1932.

Roy, M.N., *Our Differences*, Saraswati Library, Calcutta, 1938.

Roy, M.N., *Fascism: Its Philosophy, Profession and Practice,* D.M. Library, Calcutta, 1938.

Roy, M.N., *Science and Superstition,* The Renaissance Association Limited, Dehra Dun, 1940.

Roy, M.N., *Gandhism, Nationalism and Socialism,* Bengal Radical Club, Calcutta, 1940.

Roy, M.N., *Scientific Politics,* Renaissance Publishers, Calcutta, 1942.

Roy, M.N., *War and Revolution,* The Radical Democratic Party, 1942.

Roy, M.N., *The Communist International,* Radical Democratic Party Publication, Bombay, 1943.

Roy, M.N., *Nationalism: An Antiquated Cult,* Radical Democratic Party, Bombay, 1943.

Roy, M.N., *Nationalism, Democracy and Feedom,* Radical Democratic Party, Bombay, 1943.

Roy, M.N., *Planning A New India,* Renaissance Publishers, Calcutta, 1943.

Roy, M.N., *Constitution of Free India—A Draft,* Radical Democratic Party, Delhi, 1945.

Roy, M.N., *The Problems of Freedom,* Renaissance Publishers, Calcutta, 1945.

Roy, M.N., *New Orientation,* Renaissance Publishers, Calcutta, 1946.

Roy, M.N., *New Humanism: A Manifesto,* Renaissance Publishers, Calcutta, 1947.

Roy, M.N., *Radical Humanism,* Eastern Economist Pamphlets, New Delhi, 1952.

Roy, M.N., *Reason, Romanticism and Revolution,* 2 Vols., Renaissance Publishers, Calcutta, 1952.

Roy, M.N., *Politics, Power and Parties,* Renaissance Publishers, Calcutta, 1960.

Roy, M.N., *M.N. Roy's Memoirs,* Allied Publishers, Bombay, 1964.

Roy, M.N., *The Future of Socialism,* Renaissance Publishers, Calcutta, 1943.

Roy, M.N., *Future of Democracy in India*, Radical Democratic Party, Delhi.

Roy, M.N., *Humanist Politics*, Renaissance Publishers, Calcutta.

Roy, S., *The Restless Brahmin, Early Life of M.N. Roy*, Allied Publishers, Bombay, 1970.

Sampurnanand, *Indian Socialism*, Asia Publishing House, Bombay, 1961.

Saxena, K., *Modern Indian Political Thought: Gandhism and Roy's New Humanism*, Chetna Publications, New Delhi, 1978.

Sharma, B.S., *Political Philosophy of M.N. Roy*, National Publishing House, Delhi, 1965.

Shiviah, M., *New Humanism and Democratic Politics: A Study of M.N. Roy's Theory of the State*, Popular Prakashan, Bombay, 1977.

Shingh, U., *Economic Thought of Indian Socialists*, Deep & Deep Publications, New Delhi, 1985.

Singh, B., *The Political Ideas of M.N. Roy and Jayaprakash Narayan*, Ashish Publishing House, New Delhi, 1985.

Talwar, S., *Political Ideas of M.N. Roy*, Khosla Publishing House, Delhi, 1978.

Verma, V.P., *Modern Indian Political Thought*, Lakshmi Narayan Agrawal, Agra, 1967.

INDEX